Live
Like a
King

BOOKS BY WARREN W. WIERSBE

Classic Sermons on the Apostle Peter

Classic Sermons on the Attributes of God

Classic Sermons on the Birth of Christ

Classic Sermons on Christian Service

Classic Sermons on the Cross of Christ

Classic Sermons on Faith and Doubt

Classic Sermons on Family and Home

Classic Sermons on Heaven and Hell

Classic Sermons on Hope

Classic Sermons on Judas Iscariot

Classic Sermons on the Names of God

Classic Sermons on the Miracles of Jesus

Classic Sermons on Overcoming Fear

Classic Sermons on Praise

Classic Sermons on Prayer

Classic Sermons on the Prodigal Son

Classic Sermons on the Resurrection of Christ

Classic Sermons on Revival and Renewal

Classic Sermons on the Second Coming and
   Other Prophetic Themes

Classic Sermons on the Sovereignty of God

Classic Sermons on Spiritual Warfare

Classic Sermons on Suffering

Classic Sermons on Worship

Live Like a King: Developing a Royal Lifestyle from the Beatitudes

Run with the Winners: Developing a Championship
   Lifestyle from Hebrews 11

Treasury of the World's Great Sermons

Live Like a King

Developing a Royal Lifestyle from the Beatitudes

Warren W. Wiersbe

kregel
PUBLICATIONS

Grand Rapids, MI 49501

Live Like a King: Developing a Royal Lifestyle from the Beatitudes by Warren W. Wiersbe.

Copyright © 1976 by Warren W. Wiersbe.

Published in 1995 by Kregel Publications, a division of Kregel, Inc., P. O. Box 2607, Grand Rapids, MI 49501. Kregel Publications provides trusted, biblical publications for Christian growth and service. Your comments and suggestions are valued.

Cover Photograph: Photodisc
Cover Design: Alan G. Hartman

Library of Congress Cataloging-in-Publication Data
Wiersbe, Warren W.
Live Like a King: Developing a Royal Lifestyle from the Beatitudes / Warren W. Wiersbe.
    p.   cm.
  Originally published: Chicago: Moody Press, 1976.
  1. Beatitudes. I. Title.
BT382.W53   1995   226.9'306—dc20   94-37814
                                              CIP

ISBN 0-8254-3996-5 (paperback)

1 2 3 4 5 Printing / Year 99 98 97 96 95

Printed in the United States of America

My wife and I have enjoyed the fellowship of many friends in the ministry, and with affection and appreciation I dedicate this book to some of them:

Jim and Betty Gurley
Joe and Dorothy Guthrie
Gaylard and Ruth Hamilton
Bruce and Verla Love
Ken and Thelma McQuere
Pete and Alice Quist

Even as it is meet for me to think this of you all, because I have you in my heart.

(Philippians 1:7)

Contents

Preface

These chapters are based on a series of messages I delivered at Moody Church during the summer of 1975. Many who heard them expressed a desire to have them in permanent form. However, let me hasten to point out that in these chapters I have taken a somewhat different approach from the original sermons. I wish now I could preach the series again!

I recognize the fact that the Sermon on the Mount has both present and future implications. It is the former that are emphasized here. In the entire series of studies, I have tried to help the believer today realize what it means to "reign in life" through Jesus Christ. I believe that God wants each of His children to live like a king, and that the Beatitudes help point the way to that experience.

Knowing the imperfections of both the author and the book, I tremble as I send these pages forth. But if they help some believer enter more fully into the privileges of the throne, then I will consider the work rewarded. "Brethren, I count not myself to have apprehended" (Philippians 3:13).

1

Are You Walking or Riding?

Imagine what it would be like to present King Solomon on a TV show. He was "wiser than all men" (1 Kings 4:31) and was the composer of more than a thousand songs and the author of three thousand proverbs. (Imagine the books and records he could sell!) He could intelligently discuss trees, animals, birds, insects, and fish; and he was no ignoramus when it came to buildings, horses, money, or (sad to say) women. He was a keen observer of the world around him and was able to draw wisdom from events that would appear insignificant to other people.

One day he looked out his window and saw some travelers going by, some walking and some riding horses. He wrote in his journal: "There is an evil which I have seen under the sun, as an error which proceedeth from the ruler: folly is set in great dignity, and the rich sit in low place. I have seen servants upon horses, and princes walking as servants upon the earth" (Ecclesiastes 10:5-7).

Princes are supposed to ride on horses, and their servants are supposed to walk beside them. But Solomon saw the situation reversed: those who were supposed to serve were ruling, and those who were supposed to rule were serving! The world was topsy-turvy—and it still is today.

Take, for example, the marvelous machine we call the human body. God made it to be the servant of the spirit, but in the lives of many people it is the master. The appetites ride on horseback while the spirit trudges along on foot. The same reverse situation exists when it comes to money and material things. God gave them to us to be our servants, but somehow they have become our masters.

In other words, too many people are walking when they should be riding.

God created us to be kings and everything else to be our servants. The fact that we are created in the image of God is proof enough of this statement. But God's words to the first man and woman make our kingship even more exciting: "Be fruitful, and multiply, and replenish the earth, and subdue it: and have dominion over the fish of the sea, and over the fowl of the air, and over every living thing that moveth upon the earth" (Genesis 1:28). "Have dominion" means "live like a king!" Our first parents were not simply tenants in paradise; they were the rulers!

"If God created us to be kings," you may be asking at this point, "then what happened? Man certainly doesn't have dominion over the fish and fowl and animals today. For that matter, he doesn't even have dominion over *himself*."

Good question. What did happen so that man stopped living like a king and started living like a servant? When did he get off the horse and start walking? *When he disobeyed God.* When Adam and Eve deliberately disobeyed God's commandment, they went from sovereigns to sinners to servants. They lost their crowns. They got off the horse and started walking, and they became the servants instead of the rulers. And every child of Adam (and that means each one of us) is born a slave.

Can we do anything to change the situation? Yes. For just as God the Father created us to be kings, God the Son redeemed us to be kings. In His death, burial, and resurrection, Jesus Christ undid all that Adam's sin accomplished—and much more! The dominion that was lost through Adam's disobedience has been regained through Christ's obedience, and there is no longer any need for you and me to be walking like servants. Romans 5:17 puts it beautifully: "For if by one man's [Adam's] offence death reigned by one; much more they which receive abundance of grace and of the gift of righteousness shall reign in life by one, Jesus Christ."

Note those key words: "they . . . shall reign in life." Who shall reign in life? Those who have received God's free gift of grace and righteousness in Jesus Christ. And it does not say "reign in death" or "reign in the future kingdom." It says *reign in life!* That means living like a king right here and now.

In my ministry I have met many slaves who have become kings by yielding themselves to Jesus Christ. I remember Harry, who, with his wife, stopped at the church study one Friday afternoon. He was a church member, but he was also an alcoholic. Nobody knew it except Harry and his wife and a few close drinking pals. This had been going on for years. Harry would work hard at his job all week and never touch a drop. Then Friday night would arrive, and he would take off for the tavern. He would be "under the influence" all that night and all day Saturday, and would sober up in time to be in Sunday school Sunday morning.

"I'm sick of it," he told me. "Tell me what to do."

I told him what to do: "Harry, you've got to turn yourself over to Jesus Christ and let Him be the Lord of your life."

He did it—and the change was immediate! He got back on the horse and started living like a king. And not only that, but he devoted himself to helping other men find their true kingship in Jesus Christ. Whenever I was called upon by anybody having problems with alcohol, I always sent him to Harry, because he could help him better than I could. The last I heard, Harry was still riding on the horse, and his body was his servant instead of his master.

God the Father created you to be a king, God the Son redeemed you to be a king, and God the Spirit can empower you to be a king. We "reign in life" through the power of the Spirit of God. "For it is God which worketh in you both to will and to do of his good pleasure" (Philippians 2:13). "Now unto him that is able to do exceeding abundantly above all that we ask or think, according to the power that worketh in us" (Ephesians 3:20). If left to ourselves, we fail; but if we yield to the indwelling Holy Spirit, we succeed. He alone can empower us to live like kings.

The question you must answer is, Am I walking or riding? Or, to put it another way, Am I serving my servants, or are they serving me? Are you ruling over the appetites of the body? Are you in control of money and material things? (Money is a wonderful servant but a terrible master.) Are you reigning in life?

You can.

This is what the Beatitudes are all about. They explain how you can reign in life and live like a king. Most people think of the Beatitudes as a collection of idealistic sayings—beautiful to read but impossible to practice. How wrong they are! In fact, the entire Sermon on the Mount is a glorious explanation of what life is really like when you reign through the power of the Holy Spirit. Dr. G. Campbell Morgan called the Sermon on the Mount "The Manifesto of the King"—and that is just what it is. Jesus Christ the King is telling us how to live like kings! He is explaining how to reign over such servants as *ego,* so that you practice humility and not pride; *power*, so that you build up and do not destroy; *appetite*, so that you crave purity and not sin. The Beatitudes tell you how to get back in the saddle so that you are riding like a king and not trudging like a slave.

Believe me, you *can* live like a king—provided you know Jesus Christ as your Savior and completely yield to Him. We "reign in life by one, Jesus Christ" (Romans 5:17). Jesus Christ is the only king that God will recognize. Jesus was born a king; "Where is he that is born King of the Jews?" (Matthew 2:2). He lived as a king in spite of the opposition of wicked men and Satan himself.

Since Adam, Jesus Christ is the only man to walk this earth and exercise the kind of dominion that God originally gave us when He created us. For example, Jesus had dominion over the fish of the sea. He gave Peter a great catch of fish when it seemed impossible to catch anything (Luke 5:1-11); He even brought one fish to Peter's hook when the apostle had to pay his Temple tax (Matthew 17:24-27). Jesus also had dominion over the fowl of the air. He kept every bird in Jerusalem quiet until the cock was supposed to crow, announcing Peter's denial of Christ. Jesus even had dominion over the beasts of the field. During His temptation, He was in the wilderness "with the wild beasts" (Mark 1:13). And He rode into Jerusalem on a colt "whereon never man sat" (Mark 11:2). Jesus Christ is the last Adam, exercising the dominion lost by the disobedience of the first Adam—and He wants to share that dominion with you and me!

Jesus Christ was born a king, He lived as a king, and He died as a king. True, the only crown He wore was a mocking crown of thorns. And His only throne was a cross bearing the inscription "This is the King of the Jews." To human eyes, His crucifixion seemed like defeat; but to the King it meant victory. His supreme act of sovereignty was laying down His life for the sins of the world. He was not murdered; He willingly gave His life as your substitute and mine. Never was His kingship more evident than in Gethsemane and at Golgotha, where He was "obedient unto death, even the death of the cross" (Philippians 2:8). The greatest test of our kingship is how we use our authority. Jesus used His authority to save others, even though it meant He could not save Himself.

Today Jesus Christ reigns as king, for God "raised him from the dead, and set him at his own right hand in the heavenly places, far above all" (Ephesians 1:20-21). "For he must reign, till he hath put all enemies under his feet" (1 Corinthians 15:25).

The tragedy is that too many people echo that rebellious cry of centuries ago: "We will not have this man to reign over us" (Luke 19:14). This rebellion is the explanation for the problems in our world today: men believe they are free when in reality they are slaves. "The kings of the earth set themselves, and the rulers take counsel together, against the Lord, and against his anointed, saying, Let us break their bands asunder, and cast away their cords from us" (Psalm 2:2-3). But in rejecting Christ and refusing to submit to God's Word, men are only forfeiting their own kingship. We reign in life by submitting to the authority of God. George Matheson expressed it perfectly:

> My will is not my own
> Til Thou hast made it Thine;
> If it would reach the monarch's throne
> It must its crown resign.

God the Father created you to be a king, and you cannot enjoy the fulfillment of your life until you experience this kingship through Jesus Christ. God the Son redeemed you to be a king, but you cannot reign in life until He is your Savior and Lord. God the Spirit can enable you to live like a king, but His power is limited until you yield your all to Him. Your kingship depends on your relationship to God, and your relationship to God depends on the decision of your own will.

"I have seen servants upon horses, and princes walking as servants upon the earth."

You were meant to be a king.

Are you walking or riding?

2

The King Is Here!

The Beatitudes are part of what we call the Sermon on the Mount, and the Sermon on the Mount is a part of the gospel of Matthew, the "gospel of the King." If we are going to understand the message of the Beatitudes, then we are going to have to know something about both the gospel of Matthew and the Sermon on the Mount. Matthew 1:1 is a key verse: "The book of the generation of Jesus Christ, the son of David, the son of Abraham."

The Old Testament is "the book of the generations of Adam" (Genesis 5:1), and, of course, Adam was the first king in human history. God blessed Adam and gave him "dominion over the fish of the sea, and over the fowl of the air, and over every living thing that moveth upon the earth" (Genesis 1:28). But no man has a right to rule over others who cannot rule over himself. That explains why God tested Adam; for if Adam was to be God's king, he had to be *under* authority before he could *exercise* authority.

19

Adam failed, and his sin plunged the human race into depravity and death. When you read "the book of the generations of Adam," you find failure in generation after generation. Abraham lied about his wife, and so did his son, Isaac. Jacob was a schemer, and Moses was a murderer. David was an adulterer and a murderer. And these men were the spiritual leaders of the Jewish nation! No wonder the Old Testament ends with the ominous words "lest I come and smite the earth with a curse" (Malachi 4:6).

What a relief it is to turn to the gospel of Matthew and enter a new book, "the book of the generation of Jesus Christ, the son of David, the son of Abraham" (Matthew 1:1). Here is God's new king! And unlike the first Adam, Jesus Christ, the "last Adam" (1 Corinthians 15:45), obeyed God and was therefore able to exercise dominion. Because He was under authority, He was able to exercise authority. The first Adam was tested in a beautiful garden and failed; but the Last Adam was tested in a dangerous wilderness, and He succeeded. Because the first Adam was a thief, he was cast out of Paradise; but the Last Adam turned to a thief on a cross and said, "To day shalt thou be with me in paradise" (Luke 23:43). "The book of the generations of Adam" ends with a curse; but the "book of the generation of Jesus Christ" ends with the promise "There shall be no more curse" (Revelation 22:3).

You and I were born the first time into "the generations of Adam," and that made us sinners and slaves. When you are born again through faith in Jesus Christ, you enter "the generation of Jesus Christ," and you are born a child of God *and a king!* "Unto him that loved us, and washed us from our sins in his own blood, and hath made us kings and priests unto God and his Father" (Revelation 1:5-6). Because we belong to the family of the

King, we can "reign in life by one, Jesus Christ" (Romans 5:17).

The gospel of Matthew presents Jesus Christ as God's king. In the first ten chapters, Matthew answers the three questions most people would ask about a king: Where did he come from? What does he believe? What can he do? In Matthew 1-4, the *person* of the King is presented—His background, birth, baptism, and temptation. In those chapters we are assured that Jesus Christ is the Son of God, sent by the Father to be the Savior of the world. In Matthew 5-7, the Sermon on the Mount, we have the *principles* of the King—what He believes and what He wants to do in our lives. Chapters 8-10 reveal the *power* of the King and show us our Lord's power over demons, disease, and even death. In other words, in Jesus Christ we have the perfect king! When you trust Him as your Savior, He sets you free from sin and judgment, and He enables you to reign in life and enjoy His spiritual kingdom here and now.

A New Kingdom

But what kind of a kingdom do we share as we yield to Christ and reign in life? The answer to that question is given in the Sermon on the Mount. It is unfortunate that this magnificent sermon has been robbed of its importance by people applying it only to the Jews or only to some future period in God's prophetic plan. It is my conviction that the Sermon on the Mount applies to Christians today—and only to Christians. To apply it to unsaved nations is to twist the Scriptures; and to move it into some future age is to rob it of its spiritual power today. I might add that the purpose of the Sermon on the Mount is not evangelism, although certainly the Spirit could use it to give light to a seeking sinner. (I have a Jewish friend who was converted reading the genealogy in

Matthew 1, but I do not recommend you add that chapter to your tools for soul winning!) The Sermon on the Mount was given to explain to the disciples the kind of kingdom Jesus wants to build in the lives of His followers.

When our Lord began His ministry, there were several groups in Palestine that claimed to have the answer to Israel's problems. The Pharisees claimed that the nation could experience freedom and blessing only if the people returned to the traditions of the fathers. The Sadducees, on the other hand, urged the people to update their religion and become more liberal. The Essenes taught that salvation would come only through separation from the world, so they established their own communities and remained outside the life of the nation. At the other extreme were the Zealots, a revolutionary group that sought to overthrow Rome by revolt and force. Unwilling to wait for gradual change, the Zealots murdered and destroyed in the name of Jewish patriotism.

If you look deeply enough, you will see that we have similar groups today. We have those who cry, "Go back!" and attempt to return us to "the good old days" of our fathers. Another group cries, "Go ahead!" and urges us to modernize and liberalize our religion and our philosophy of life. The radical extremists shout, "Go against!" and try to destroy vital institutions necessary for the strength and progress of society. The separatists say, "Go out!" and isolate themselves from the very people who may need their help. The names of the groups will change from generation to generation, but the basic aims are the same.

In contrast to all of these solutions to the human problem is what Jesus calls the kingdom of God or the kingdom of heaven. (Matthew seemed to prefer "kingdom of heaven," probably because his Jewish readers would be afraid to pronounce the name of God.) In the Sermon on the Mount Jesus in effect says, "All of these approaches are right in some respects and wrong in other respects. Their chief weakness is that they are fragmentary: they each deal with a fact of truth but not with the whole of truth."

For example, there is nothing wrong with the tradition of the fathers. But the Old Testament law was temporary; it was preparation for the coming of the Messiah, Jesus Christ. We cannot duplicate the religion of Israel under the Old Covenant. Instead, we must let this Old Testament truth develop into New Testament truth through Jesus Christ. That is why Jesus said, "Think not that I am come to destroy the law, or the prophets: I am not come to destroy, but to fulfil" (Matthew 5:17). The Old Testament law was the seed; the gospel of Christ is the fruit. You can destroy a seed by pulverizing it with a hammer or by planting it in the ground and letting it fulfill its purpose by becoming a plant. It destroys itself by fulfilling itself. This is how Jesus Christ fulfilled the law: He brought it to its fruition in His life, death, and resurrection; and now "the righteousness of the law [is] fulfilled in us, who walk not after the flesh, but after the Spirit" (Romans 8:4).

If the Pharisees wanted to hold on to the past and reject the present, the Sadducees went to the other extreme: they wanted to take the rational approach to life and sacrifice the authority of the Word on the altar of intellectual credibility. They were the modernists of their day. Jesus agreed with them that the Word must be a living reality today, but He rejected their anti-supernatural approach. "For the Sadducees say that there is no resurrection, neither angel, nor spirit" (Acts 23:8). When the Sadducees tried to trip Him up with their theological questions, Jesus swept them aside with one devastating statement: "Ye do err, not knowing the scriptures, nor the power of God" (Matthew 22:29). It is through the Word of

God and the power of God by His Spirit that the believer today experiences the reign of God in his life. The Pharisees lost the present by trying to return to the past. The Sadducees lost the present by denying the past. Both were wrong.

Jesus would have sympathized with the Essenes in their desire for holy living, but He would have rejected their isolationism. If the Sermon on the Mount emphasizes anything, it is that sin is a matter of the heart and not merely outward actions. One does not have to murder to be a sinner; he only has to hate (Matthew 5:21-26). And he can carry a hateful heart into the desert wastes with him! Years ago, a religious college announced in its catalog: "Our campus is located forty miles from any known sin." What a preposterous claim! The Sermon on the Mount emphasizes holy living—but not at the expense of the normal duties and demands of human life. A change in geography is no guarantee of an improvement in character.

As for the Zealots, Jesus chose one of their number to be one of His disciples: "Simon called Zelotes" (Luke 6:15). Imagine selecting a political fanatic to be among the first disciples! No doubt Jesus admired their zeal and devotion, just as He certainly opposed their violent methods. He would say to Simon, "Yes, some things in 'the establishment' need to be destroyed—but not through hatred, violence, and human force. The weapons we use are not of the flesh; they are of the Spirit. It is not by killing others but by being willing to die yourself that you will establish God's kingdom."

The Sermon on the Mount has for its theme our Lord's statement in Matthew 5:20: "For I say unto you, That except your righteousness shall exceed the righteousness of the scribes, and Pharisees, ye shall in no case enter into the kingdom of heaven."

A New Righteousness

What was wrong with the righteousness of the scribes and Pharisees? For one thing, they believed that holiness was only a matter of outward actions, and they ignored the inward attitudes of the heart. Their righteousness was only external, a safe system of dos and don'ts by which they could measure their spirituality. In one of His parables, Jesus had the Pharisee pray: "I thank thee, that I am not as other men are, extortioners, unjust, adulterers, or even as this publican. I fast twice in the week, I give tithes of all that I possess" (Luke 18:11-12). Certainly there is nothing good about being an extortioner or an adulterer, and there is nothing bad about fasting or tithing. But if that is the whole of a man's religion, he has nothing! And if he is proud of it to the point of looking down upon a fellow sinner, then he is in bad condition spiritually!

In the Beatitudes Jesus teaches us that true righteousness is a matter of the heart. It has been well said, "The Beatitudes describe the *attitudes* that ought to *be* in the believer's life." What good are tithing, fasting, and outward obedience to rules and regulations if the heart is proud, critical, and condemning? Conduct must be based upon character. "For man looketh on the outward appearance, but the Lord looketh on the heart" (1 Samuel 16:7). "Keep thy heart with all diligence; for out of it are the issues of life" (Proverbs 4:23).

In Matthew 5:21-48 Jesus illustrates this basic principle that righteousness must be a matter of the heart. He takes some of the traditions of the elders and shows they are inadequate. "Thou shalt not kill" involves much more than physical violence: hatred in the heart is the equivalent of murder with the hand. "Thou shalt not commit adultery" involves much more than an immoral act: cultivating the desire in the heart is the equivalent of adultery.

The Sermon on the Mount goes much deeper than the Ten Commandments; for, with one exception ("Thou shalt not covet"), the Ten Commandments deal only with outward actions, whereas the Sermon on the Mount deals with inward attitudes. In the Sermon on the Mount, Jesus not only breaks away the shell of Pharisaic tradition that covered God's law, but He also penetrates to the heart of that law and explains its deeper, spiritual meaning. The Word of God is like seed. The Pharisees put a "crust" of tradition around the seed so that it could not give life and bear fruit. Jesus breaks that crust and then opens the husk of the seed so the spiritual life can be fulfilled in us.

The Beatitudes, then, are a description of true righteousness in contrast to the false righteousness of the scribes and Pharisees. If we are going to live like kings, then we must manifest this kind of character; and we can do it only through the power of the Holy Spirit. Interestingly enough, the Holy Spirit is not even mentioned in these chapters; yet it is obvious that the believer could never in his own power attain this high level of Christian experience. "For what the law could not do, in that it was weak through the flesh, God sending his own Son in the likeness of sinful flesh, and for sin, condemned sin in the flesh: that the righteousness of the law might be fulfilled in us, who walk not after the flesh, but after the Spirit" (Romans 8:3-4).

Not only were the Pharisees and scribes mistaken about righteousness and sin, but they were also mistaken in their motives for serving God; and Jesus deals with this error in Matthew 6. The Pharisees and scribes were religious in order to get the approval and praise of man. But the true Christian has a greater motive than that: he lives for the approval and praise of God. After all, if true righteousness is a matter of the heart, and only God can see the heart, then only God can give the reward. "I am he which searcheth the reins and hearts" (Revelation 2:23).

Jesus warns us in Matthew 6 not to "do righteousness" —whether it be giving, fasting, or praying—in order to be seen of men. He says, "Live your life before the eye of God, not the eyes of men. Your Father sees in secret, and that is sufficient. If you live for the praise of men, you have your reward."

The Beatitudes, then, are God's description of Christian character, the kind of character that leads to right conduct. When the Pharisee wondered because Jesus did not go through the ceremonial washing of hands at dinner, Jesus said to him: "Now you Pharisees have the habit of cleaning the outside of your cups and dishes, but inside you yourselves are full of greed and wickedness. You fools! Did not the One who made the outside make the inside too? But dedicate once for all your inner self, and at once you will have everything clean" (Luke 11:39-41, Williams). If there is dirty water coming out of the faucet, I do not buy a new faucet—I cleanse the cistern.

A New Challenge

In this book, we will consider the Beatitudes individually; but there is truth to be gained by first considering them collectively. To begin with, the Beatitudes show us how to enter the kingdom. The first step is admitting my spiritual bankruptcy and having a humble, honest attitude toward myself. "Blessed are the poor in spirit" applies the ax to the very root of pharisaical pride and hypocrisy. "Blessed are they that mourn" deals with my attitude toward my sin: instead of criticizing the other person, I judge myself. "Blessed are the meek" deals with my attitude toward God: I am submissive to Him and not trying to impress Him with who I am or what I have done. When I "hunger and thirst after righteousness," then God provides that righteousness in the person of His Son, Jesus Christ. Like the Pharisee Saul of Tarsus, I exchange my own self-righteousness for the grace-righteousness of Christ (Philippians 3:1-11).

But this is more than a commercial transaction, for the results can be seen in everyday life. Having received the righteousness of Christ, I can begin to manifest in my life the very character of God. I become merciful instead of condemning; I seek to cultivate purity of heart; I become a peacemaker, not a troublemaker. As I grow to become more like Christ, I experience the kind of treatment He received when He was on earth—reviling, persecution, false accusations. But because of His grace, I become salt and light in a world that is decayed and dark. Having entered the kingdom, it is now my privilege to enlarge the kingdom by applying His righteousness in the world about me.

This means that the Beatitudes are practically meaningless to the person who has never trusted Jesus Christ as Savior. They may illustrate an ideal, but that ideal can never be reached in human strength alone. But the person who begins with "Blessed are the poor in spirit" should ultimately come to that place of trusting the Savior. "To this man will I look," says the Lord, "even to him that is poor and of a contrite spirit, and trembleth at my word" (Isaiah 66:2).

The Beatitudes tell us how to enter the kingdom and enlarge the kingdom; but they also tell us how to enjoy the kingdom. "Blessed are . . . for they shall . . ." They shall *what?* Just read the promises, and you will see how much the believer enjoys from God when he seeks to cultivate true Christian character. "Theirs is the kingdom"—authority. "They shall be comforted"—encouragement. "They shall inherit the earth"—provision for every need. "They shall be filled"—satisfaction. "They shall obtain mercy"—provision for ministry to others. "They shall see God"—spiritual vision. "They shall be called the children of God"—becoming more like God in daily life. There is a price to pay, but the results are well worth it.

Jesus Christ invites you and me into a life of enrichment and enlargement.

Will you and I pay the price?

Blessed are the poor in spirit: for theirs is the kingdom of heaven.

(Matthew 5:3)

Except ye be converted, and become as little children, ye shall not enter into the kingdom of heaven.

(Matthew 18:3)

Every one that exalteth himself shall be abased; and he that humbleth himself shall be exalted.

(Luke 18:14)

Humble yourselves therefore under the mighty hand of God, that he may exalt you in due time.

(1 Peter 5:6)

God resisteth the proud, but giveth grace unto the humble.

(James 4:6)

3

The Poor in Spirit

CONFUSION

What does it mean to be "poor in spirit?"

Most assuredly, it does not mean being poor-spirited. Unfortunately, there are some people who have little or no self-esteem and whose self-image is poor; as a consequence, their inner man is anemic.

I once counseled a young man who, during childhood, had heard nothing from his father but, "You are good for nothing and will never amount to anything!" The young man had such a low opinion of himself that he failed in everything he attempted, and every failure only added to his emotional and spiritual bankruptcy. I pointed out to him that he was important to God and therefore ought to have more self-esteem. After all, he was created in the image of God. Even more, Jesus Christ died for Him, and the Holy Spirit lived in him—so he was worth something! All of this theology he accepted with his mind, but down in his heart he could still hear his father telling him how worthless he was.

Some people are shy and retiring by nature, but that is not the same as being poor in spirit. God created us with different temperaments and personalities; and some of us are extroverts, whereas others are introverts. But it is possible to be an introvert and proud or an extrovert and humble. Peter was certainly an extrovert, and Thomas probably an introvert; yet Thomas's refusal to accept the fact of Christ's resurrection—and his demand for proof—was just as much an evidence of pride as Peter's boasting and poor swordsmanship. Shyness is not poverty of spirit.

Neither is the detestable, groveling attitude that we call mock humility. The classic example is Uriah Heep in *David Copperfield*, who was always reminding people that he was "but a very 'umble person." In a more refined way, we see this mock humility in the person who denies about himself what everybody else knows is true. I once worked with a Sunday school teacher who had a great gift of working with children, yet she would deny it every time it was mentioned. "Oh, I can't do anything!" she would protest. "I just struggle along until somebody comes to do the job the way it ought to be done!" All of us in the meetings would smile at each other and change the subject. We knew that her "protesting too much" was a veiled request for praise, and none of us felt like praising her.

In a sense Moses was guilty of this sin when he told God he was not able to speak. Who can tell God anything about himself that God does not already know? And, after all, God made us, and God is able to empower us to do whatever He calls us to do. Denying that we can accomplish God's work is not humility; it is the worst kind of pride!

Being poor in spirit means knowing yourself, accepting yourself, and being yourself to the glory of God.

It means *knowing* yourself—your strengths and weaknesses, your hidden desires, your ambitions, your spiritual gifts and natural abilities—and being honest with yourself. When I was in grade school, I almost developed an emotional disorder over sports. Both of my older brothers are capable athletes, but I am not; and every single time the boys in my class chose sides, I was the last one chosen. At first it was a painful experience. After all, every schoolboy dreams of being a great baseball or football star. Then it got to be a joke, and finally I was able to accept the fact that I would never be a great athlete—or even a good player. One of my coaches was sure he could make a trackman out of me, but after I knocked down six hurdles and fractured my ankle, he changed his mind. Sometimes getting to know yourself can be a painful experience, but it is a part of maturing.

It also means *accepting* yourself. Some people, when they discover what they really are, deny their discovery and move into a life of pretending. In fact, some people have pretended their way right into a dream world of psychological problems and have completely lost touch with reality. Most of us do not go that far, but the inability to accept yourself can have serious emotional and spiritual consequences. When you accept yourself, you find it easier to accept others and also easier to accept God's plan for your life. It did not take me long to accept the fact that I was neither an athlete nor a mechanic. (I handle a hammer about as well as I do a baseball bat.) But early in grade school I discovered a flair for words, and I have been speaking them and writing them ever since.

Being poor in spirit means knowing yourself, accepting yourself, and *being* yourself to the glory of God—your best self, of course, and not anything less. That means constant growing in every area of your life. It means using your strengths to overcome your weaknesses and using your weaknesses to discover the mighty power of God. "When I am weak, then am I strong" (2 Corinthians

12:10). Being yourself involves yielding to the Spirit of God and permitting Him to fulfill God's will in your life. You are not imitating somebody else or envying somebody else. You are yourself—your best self—empowered by the Spirit of God to do what God has called you to do.

To be poor in spirit means knowing that in myself I am bankrupt, but in Christ I am rich. It means discovering the place God wants me to fill and filling it for His glory, no matter how insignificant or unimportant I may believe it is. The person who is truly poor in spirit knows that *every* place of God's choosing is an important place. "The eye cannot say unto the hand, I have no need of thee: nor again the head to the feet, I have no need of you" (1 Corinthians 12:21). The believer who is poor in spirit is in the place of God's choosing, fulfilling the purpose of God's choosing and depending on the power that God alone can supply.

Perhaps the word *humility* is another way of saying "poor in spirit." I believe it was Andrew Murray who said that humility is that grace that, when you know you have it, you have lost it! He also said, "Humility is not thinking meanly of yourself. It is simply not thinking of yourself at all!" This explains why "blessed are the poor in spirit" is the first of the Beatitudes; for until we admit our need we can never receive what God has for us. Too many people are like those in the Laodicean church; they are "rich, and increased with goods, and have need of nothing" (Revelation 3:17). And, like the Laodiceans, they know not that they are "wretched, and miserable, and poor, and blind, and naked."

To be poor in spirit does not mean to deny your personality or try to suppress it. It simply means yielding it to God for Him to make it all that He wants it to be. The motto is old but true: "God always gives His best to those who leave the choice with Him."

CHARACTERISTICS

There are several evidences of humility in the life of the believer. To begin with, when you are poor in spirit, you *accept others, because you have accepted yourself.* That does not mean you always agree with what they are or what they do, but you accept them just the same. When others succeed you are happy for them; when they fail you try to encourage them. If I find myself happy when they fail and sad when they succeed, then I am not poor in spirit. I am proud. When young David killed Goliath, King Saul was glad to get rid of his enemy and honor David; but when David started slaying his ten thousands in contrast to Saul's thousands, then the king became envious and angry. David was poor in spirit: "Who am I? and what is my life, or my father's family in Israel, that I should be son in law to the king?" (1 Samuel 18:18). At no time did David use his position to promote himself; he was willing for God to do the promoting, in His time and in His way. "David behaved himself wisely in all his ways; and the Lord was with him" (1 Samuel 18:14).

A constant source of friction among the disciples—and it must have grieved their Master's heart—was, "Who is the greatest in the kingdom of heaven?" (Matthew 18:1). Our Lord's answer was to place an unspoiled child in their midst. Why is an unspoiled child great, so much so that men will risk their lives to protect and save him? He is great because he knows he is a child and acts like a child. When a child starts acting like an adult, he becomes disgusting and offensive. (Perhaps the only thing worse is an adult acting like a child.) But when a child naturally acts like a child, he is a beautiful thing to behold, and you cannot help but love him. A child without guile or affectation is the king—all the world bows before his little throne!

King Saul could not become like a little child and, as a result, lost his crown, his kingdom, and his life. He pretended to be something that he was not. Samuel commanded him to wait for the prophet's arrival before any sacrifices were offered, but Saul could not wait. He pretended to be a priest (1 Samuel 13:5-14), and he impetuously offered the sacrifice. Later, when God gave him another chance and commanded him to exterminate the Amalekites, Saul pretended to be God and deliberately disobeyed the orders (1 Samuel 15). The final scene in Saul's life shows the king completely abandoned by God (1 Samuel 28). He prayed but received no answers; even the dreams, the priests, and the prophets brought no message from God. So he decided to consult a witch. "Saul disguised himself," 1 Samuel 28:8 says, and went by night to a witch's cave. In one sense Saul did disguise himself; but in another sense he was revealing his true self! All along he had been rebelling against God, and "rebellion is as the sin of witchcraft" (1 Samuel 15:23). The next day Saul committed suicide on the field of battle, and his crown was taken by an Amalekite, one of the men Saul himself should have slain (2 Samuel 1:10).

Another evidence of poverty of spirit is *accepting circumstances.* When circumstances do not go my way, do I become angry and critical? Am I always trying to manipulate people and circumstances for my own benefit and comfort? Am I willing to give in to make things easier for somebody else? Do I cut corners and pull deals to accomplish what I want in life? Paul said, "I have learned, in whatsoever state I am, therewith to be content" (Philippians 4:11). That does not mean that Christians never try to improve their circumstances, because that would be complacency, not contentment. But it does mean that the poor in spirit do not chafe in uncomfortable circumstances and spend their time complaining both to God and men.

A third evidence is *a right attitude toward things.* The person who is poor in spirit does not find his satisfaction in things: he can do with or he can do without. "I know both how to be abased, and I know how to abound" (Philippians 4:12). He does not measure a man's worth by how much material wealth he owns, for "a man's life consisteth not in the abundance of the things which he possesseth" (Luke 12:15). If things change my attitudes, then things are my master, not my servant—and that is the sin of idolatry. The proud man is possessed by things; the humble man possesses things and uses them for the good of others and the glory of God.

The parable of the rich farmer illustrates this truth (Luke 12:13-21). Material wealth is either a window through which we see God or a mirror in which we see ourselves—and with this farmer it was the latter. There are eleven personal pronouns in this farmer's conversation with himself. He talks *about* himself *to* himself. And he had no thought for God or his hungry neighbor. Had he been poor in spirit he would have been rich toward God; but because he believed he was rich, he became poor and lost everything. He believed he was an owner, but he discovered (too late) that he was only a steward. God was the Owner, and all the fruits and goods were merely on loan. He possessed, but he did not own.

Thoreau was correct when he wrote, "A man is rich in proportion to the number of things which he can afford to let alone." Paul expressed it even better: "For we brought nothing into this world, and it is certain we can carry nothing out. And having food and raiment let us be therewith content" (1 Timothy 6:7-8). The man who is poor in spirit does not build his life on *things.* He has God, and that is all he needs.

Let me suggest a fourth evidence of humility: *accepting God's will for your life.* The person who is poor in spirit joyfully accepts the will of God; the proud person resists God's will. I have met people who are so proud that they even *defy* God. I remember a Christian couple who had big plans for their children and told God what He was supposed to do. He did it, and they lived to regret it. "He gave them their request; but sent leanness into their soul" (Psalm 106:15).

Sometimes God gives us seeming failure to teach us to submit to His will. I learned that lesson in a little fishing village in Denmark, where I ministered with a Youth For Christ team in 1957. I did not know the language, the people of the village did not seem interested in the gospel, and I felt like quitting. Few people were attending the services, but night after night my associate and I led the singing and preached the Word. Before the week ended, we learned that God had indeed changed some hearts—not as many as we had hoped, but far more than we deserved. During that week I learned to obey God's will in spite of my feelings and in spite of the results, a lesson I hope I never forget.

The person who is self-satisfied and self-sufficient, who feels no need for God, is not poor in spirit. The believer who argues with God's will and complains about circumstances is not poor in spirit. The person who fishes for compliments and inflates when compliments come is not poor in spirit. The leader who is harder on others than he is on himself is not poor in spirit.

To be poor in spirit, then, means to know yourself, accept yourself, and be yourself, to the glory of God. It means letting God use both your strengths and your weaknesses to accomplish His will and glorify His name.

CONSEQUENCES

Why does being poor in spirit bring blessing? An attitude of humility is exactly opposite to what the world teaches, and usually opposite to what most people practice. "Assert yourself!" is the world's slogan. But Jesus says, "Humble yourself." How can humility bring blessing to you when you live in a cutthroat world?

To begin with, humility is godlike, and anything that makes us more like God is bound to bring blessing, even if the world will not accept it. "Who is like unto the Lord our God, who dwelleth on high, who humbleth himself to behold the things that are in heaven, and in the earth!" (Psalm 113:5-6). God the Father humbles Himself to behold the things both in heaven and on earth! God the Son "humbled himself, and became obedient unto death, even the death of the cross" (Philippians 2:8). Think of the humility of the Holy Spirit as He lives with us day by day!

It is difficult to conceive of a Christian growing in grace apart from humility. True poverty of spirit is the soil out of which the fruit of the Spirit can be cultivated. "To this man will I look, even to him that is poor and of a contrite spirit, and trembleth at my word" (Isaiah 66:2). Certainly the seed of God's Word could never be planted in the hard soil of a proud heart. "Break up your fallow ground, and sow not among thorns" (Jeremiah 4:3).

But there is another reason poverty of spirit brings blessing: it makes us kings. "Blessed are the poor in spirit: for theirs is the kingdom of heaven." We control by being controlled. No man has a right to exercise authority who himself is not under authority. We reign in life by submitting to the authority of Jesus Christ (Romans 5:17).

What is involved in reigning in life? It means authority; for when we submit to Christ, He is able to share His authority with us. Pride always weakens a person, because pride cuts us off from fellowship with the Lord. Peter was his weakest when, in pride, he wielded his sword and tried to defend Jesus. Peter was his strongest when he wept bitterly, humbled himself, and submitted to Jesus. Jesus used a little child as the perfect example of a citizen of His kingdom because in a child you see authority based on humility. Because a child is so weak in himself, he commands all the strength of those about him. The world believes that authority comes from size, ability, noise, and self-promotion; the Christian knows that true authority comes from poverty of spirit. We reign as kings because we submit as servants.

This spiritual kingdom involves not only authority but also liberty. Pride always makes a slave of a person, whereas humility sets that person free. When you live to promote yourself, you are bound to become a slave of people or things or circumstances. You are never really free to be yourself, because self has already enslaved you through pride. The person who is poor in spirit is not disturbed by the attitudes or criticisms of others, because he lives to please God. Moses was not afraid of Pharaoh, because Pharaoh could do nothing to hurt God's servant so long as that servant was submitted to the Lord. When you live to promote yourself, you must always get something from others to inflate your ego or advertise your importance; but every time you receive something you pay dearly. "Honor me now, I pray thee, before the elders of my people, and before Israel" pleaded King Saul (1 Samuel 15:30). His pride made him a slave. He was not the king of Israel: Israel was king over him!

Humility means that you look to God for everything you need. This sets you free from people, circumstances, and things. If you need nothing but God, then nothing —and no one—can be a threat to you. You are free!

Humility makes us kings, not only by giving us authority and liberty but also by giving us adequacy. "The Lord killeth, and maketh alive: he bringeth down to the grave, and bringeth up. The Lord maketh poor, and maketh rich: he bringeth low, and lifteth up. He raiseth up the poor out of the dust, and lifteth up the beggar from the dunghill, to set them among princes, and to make them inherit the throne of glory" (1 Samuel 2:6-8). When we are low enough, then God can trust us with a throne and a scepter. He opens the treasures of His grace to the dead, the poor, and the beggars! His feast is spread for "the poor, and the maimed, and the halt, and the blind" (Luke 14:21), not the proud who believe their souls can be satisfied with lands, oxen, and honeymoons!

There is a poverty in riches, and there are riches in poverty. "There is that maketh himself rich, yet hath nothing: there is that maketh himself poor, yet hath great riches" (Proverbs 13:7). "For ye know the grace of our Lord Jesus Christ, that, though he was rich, yet for your sakes he became poor, that ye through his poverty might be rich" (2 Corinthians 8:9). It is a singular fact that the rich people commit suicide, whereas the poor do not. The person who depends on material things cannot reign in life, because he is possessed by the things he possesses. He is controlled by things, and he is never satisfied with the things that he has.

When you and I are poor in spirit, God gives us a kingdom, and we reign in life. When King Saul was a humble servant, God gave him a kingdom; but when Saul began to throw his weight around and run things his own way, then he lost his kingdom. How did David get his kingdom? By being a nobody. This is how Jesus Christ secured His kingdom: "Wherefore God also hath highly exalted him, and given him a name which is above every name" (Philippians 2:9). This is the paradox of the Christian life: we surrender that we might reign. This leads to authority, liberty, and adequacy.

CULTIVATION

How can we cultivate this grace of humility? How is it possible to succeed in this difficult world while seeking to be poor in spirit?

I believe the first step is to *accept God's estimate of yourself*. You had to do this to become a Christian, and you have to do this to grow in the Christian life. When Christ first confronted you with the gospel, you perhaps had a difficult time agreeing with His estimate of your life. "For all have sinned, and come short of the glory of God" (Romans 3:23). "There is none righteous, no, not one" (Romans 3:10). "Ye must be born again" (John 3:7). Once you accepted God's estimate of yourself, it was easy to accept God's remedy for your sins. You had to humble yourself, and then God lifted you up.

"For I say, through the grace given unto me, to every man that is among you, not to think of himself more highly than he ought to think; but to think soberly, according as God hath dealt to every man the measure of faith" (Romans 12:3). Paul is not suggesting that we not think of ourselves, because that would be impossible. He is warning us not to think more highly of ourselves than we ought to; and I believe we ought to include *less* highly as well. There is a false humility that degrades as much as does a proud spirit. I suggested early in this chapter that true humility means knowing myself, accepting myself, and being myself, to the glory of God. This means accepting God's estimate of me on the basis of the gifts and the faith He has given me.

For example, Moses argued with God when God called him to go to Egypt. Moses used every excuse he could find, all of them centered on his own weaknesses. Gideon made the same mistake when God called him to deliver the people from the power of Midian. Imagine God calling a fearful farmer a "mighty man of valour" (Judges 6:12)! Imagine Jesus Christ calling Simon a "rock" (Matthew 16:18)! When Moses, Gideon, and Simon accepted God's estimate and acted upon it by faith, they accomplished great things for God. They found their kingdom by humbly yielding to God and daring to believe what He said. Every victory they won was the result of their faith in God's word.

As you read your Bible, notice what God says about you as a child of God. Accept what He says, and act upon it. When Moses, Gideon, and Simon argued with the word of God, it led to defeat. When they accepted the word and acted upon it the result was victory. God does not say to us, "Obey, and I will bless you." Rather, He in effect says, "I have already blessed you with all spiritual blessings in Christ; now, draw upon this wealth, believe what I say, and live like a king!" (see Ephesians 1:3).

The second step is to *yield yourself to God daily* and draw your strength from Him. "Without me ye can do nothing" (John 15:5). Many Christians find it helpful to get up early enough in the morning to spend uninterrupted time in prayer and meditation on God's Word. What digestion is to your body, meditation is to your soul; and what food is to digestion, the Word of God is to meditation. "Man shall not live by bread alone, but by every word that proceedeth out of the mouth of God" (Matthew 4:4). The Word of God taken into your inner man releases power. The Bible is the scepter by which you reign in life. Spend time daily in quiet communion with God, and carry the power of that experience with you all through the day. We do not read that King Saul was a great man of prayer, or that he meditated on the Word; but in the Psalms, we constantly meet King David talking to God and letting God talk to him.

The Word of God will transform your mind (Romans 12:2) so that you will have "the mind of Christ"—the same attitude Jesus had when He laid aside His glory and came to earth as a servant (Philippians 2:5-7). You were not born with the attitude of a servant; you were born with the attitude of a rebel. It is only as the mind is transformed by the Word that we can ever cultivate true humility and poverty of spirit.

The third step is this: *focus on Christ and His blessings.* Too many people believe humility comes from studying their own sins and failures, but that is not true. It is not the badness of man that leads to repentance but "the goodness of God" (Romans 2:4). If you conduct too many "spiritual autopsies" you may bleed to death! There is nothing wrong with honest self-examination, *provided that you look to Christ.* However, too many Christians spend too much time looking into the mirror when they ought to be "looking unto Jesus, the author and finisher of our faith" (Hebrews 12:2). The more you contemplate the goodness of God, the lower you will sink before Him. "Who am I, O Lord God, and what is mine house, that thou hast brought me hitherto?" prayed King David (1 Chronicles 17:16).

Peter's experience with the Lord in Luke 5 is a good illustration of the truth that humility comes from contemplating God's blessings and not our own failures. Peter had fished all night and caught nothing when Jesus entered his boat and used it for a platform as He taught the multitudes. Peter was a captive audience and had to listen to the Word; but this Word was preparing him for a miracle. ("Faith cometh by hearing, and hearing by the Word of God" [Romans 10:17].) When Jesus commanded Peter to launch out into the deep, the fisherman protested weakly but obeyed, and the result was a great catch of fish. "When Simon Peter saw it, he fell down at Jesus' knees, saying, Depart from me; for I am a sinful man, O Lord!" (v. 8). It was not his night of failure that drove Peter to his knees, but the great success that Jesus gave to him! Anybody can say, "I am a sinful man!" when he has failed; but it takes an honest, humble man to say this when he has succeeded. It was the goodness of God that led Peter to repentance, and if you and I will only meditate on His goodness, we, too, will grow in humility and poverty of spirit.

Next comes the fourth step: *look for opportunities to serve others.* Humility and service go together. The proud man looks for others to serve him, whereas the humble man looks for ways to serve others. "Let each esteem other better than themselves" (Philippians 2:3). "By love serve one another" (Galatians 5:13). "Yea, and if I be offered upon the sacrifice and service of your faith, I joy, and rejoice with you all" (Philippians 2:17). Sacrifice and service are the twin children of humility. It is important to note that this sacrifice and service must go unnoticed and unrewarded. "They have their reward!" If we blow a trumpet every time we help somebody, we will only nourish our pride and starve our humility. A cup of cold water for Jesus' sake is all that He asks.

Do not look for *big* opportunities "worthy" of your abilities. Those will come in due time. The great saints of the Bible started as servants, not rulers; and they were faithful over a few things before God made them kings. Moses tended sheep; Joseph was a steward; David was a shepherd; Jesus was a carpenter. Live with the eye of God upon you, and forget the praise of men. Serve faithfully in the hidden place, and in due time God will lift you up. Every opportunity for service is an opportunity to exercise sovereignty in Christ. We reign in life by living to serve, to the glory of God.

The sin of pride has ruined more lives than perhaps any other sin. It is the sin that invites Satan to rule. It is the sin that cost King Saul his character, his crown, and, ultimately, his life. Humility is the grace that made David a king!

"Blessed are the poor in spirit: for theirs is the kingdom of heaven."

Blessed are they that mourn: for they shall be comforted.
                                                    (Matthew 5:4)

For godly sorrow worketh repentance to salvation not to be repented of: but the sorrow of the world worketh death.
                                                    (2 Corinthians 7:10)

Peter went out, and wept bitterly.
                                                    (Luke 22:62)

He [Judas] cast down the pieces of silver in the temple, and departed, and went and hanged himself.
                                                    (Matthew 27:5)

As sorrowful, yet always rejoicing.
                                                    (2 Corinthians 6:10)

He hath sent me to bind up the brokenhearted . . . to comfort all that mourn.
                                                    (Isaiah 61:1-2)

Weeping may endure for a night, but joy cometh in the morning.
                                                    (Psalm 30:5)

4

The Mourners

If you want to know a person's character, find out what makes him laugh and what makes him weep. This test is not infallible, because we all have our difficult days; but generally speaking it is true. It always amazes me when people laugh at a drunk or at a comedian impersonating a drunk. I see nothing funny in drunkenness or in drunken behavior. As a pastor I have seen too much of the tragedy of drink to be entertained by a drunk.

What we laugh at and what we weep over indicates our values of life, and values are a part of maturity. Little children will laugh at things that seem stupid to us, and they will cry over matters that seem trivial to us. I read about a terrible train accident in Great Britain that killed a number of passengers. In one of the cars was a mother with a little child in her arms, and the mother was dead but the child was unharmed. When the rescuers took the child away from the dead mother, the child laughed and played; but when they took away her candy, she broke into a terrible tantrum of weeping and screaming. The fact that her mother was dead did not bother the child, because she knew nothing about death. But she did know about candy!

That means that the higher you go in life, the more vulnerable you are in sorrow. You can escape sorrow if you wish to, simply by isolating yourself from other people and from the affairs of life; but at the same time you will also be escaping joy. For the higher you go on the scale of life, the greater the opportunities for joy; and the same things that cause joy can also cause sorrow. Animals feel pain, and some pets seem to show sorrow; but for the most part animals know nothing of a broken heart. But how many of us are willing to become animals merely to avoid sorrow? Most children know nothing of the deep hurts that bring tears to adult eyes; but how many of us would want to become children to escape the pains of adult life?

Whenever you enter into the presence of joy, you make yourself a candidate for sorrow. A young couple that marries experiences joy; but suppose she comes down with a terminal illness, or suppose he is hopelessly crippled in an accident? A couple can bring children into the world, and children are a joy; but suppose one of them develops leukemia and dies? Just about everything in life that brings joy can also be a source of sorrow; and the only way to escape that sorrow is to run away from life.

Jesus never tried to escape the sorrows of life. Neither did He deny that they existed. *He transformed them.* Jesus did not tell His disciples to go out and look for sorrow; but He did tell them that He was able to transform their tears and bring them comfort. Of itself, sorrow never makes a person better. I have seen it make people bitter. But sorrow plus Jesus Christ can bring a transforming experience of power into the life of the one who is mourning.

If you and I are to experience the comfort of God, we must understand the three different kinds of sorrow that can come to us in life.

NATURAL SORROW

First, there is *natural* sorrow. This kind of sorrow comes to everybody—saved and unsaved, rich and poor, young and old. It is a natural part of life. God made us to be able to weep. Some of the songs and sermons you hear give the impression that a Christian never weeps. But Abraham, the great man of faith, wept when his dear wife died; and David wept when his rebellious son was killed in battle. Jeremiah wept when he saw his beloved nation go into captivity. Jesus wept over the lost city of Jerusalem; He also wept at the tomb of His friend Lazarus. Jesus never wept for Himself; and He admonished the woman of Jerusalem not to weep over Him; but He did weep for others. When Paul said farewell to his dear friends from Ephesus, he wept and they wept. As you read the Bible, you get the impression that God expects His people to weep. "To every thing there is a season, and a time to every purpose under the heaven: a time to be born, and a time to die . . . a time to weep, and a time to laugh" (Ecclesiastes 3:1-2, 4).

When God created the first man, He gave him the ability to weep; and He did this *before* man had sinned. Natural weeping is not sinful. On the contrary, it is a gift from God. There is healing in natural weeping. Doctors and psychologists in the past twenty-five years have helped us to understand what really happens when we mourn, and their discoveries have helped us (with God's assistance) to heal the brokenhearted. Natural sorrow expressed in mourning releases a healing process in a person's life that enables him to accept the pain, work his way through it, and adjust to life again. In my ministry I have noticed that the people who, for one reason or another, do not mourn, do not easily adjust to new circumstances; their wounds never seem to heal.

Mourning is an expression of love. It is also a proof that the person has accepted the fact of the crisis and wants to handle it in an adult manner. When the pain is kept inside it poisons the emotional system in the same way an infection spreads through the bloodstream. I have heard well-meaning people say in funeral homes, "Now, don't cry! You know she is better off!" Don't cry? Why, the thing the person needs to do more than anything else is to cry! This is God's way of helping him release the pressure and pain inside, and it is a perfectly natural thing. Some people have the idea that weeping is a sign of weakness. Self-pity is a sign of weakness, but not weeping. Jesus was the strongest Man who ever walked on this earth, and He wept openly!

There is a hopeless sorrow that people experience who do not know Christ. "I would not have you to be ignorant, brethren, concerning them which are asleep, that ye sorrow not, even as others which have no hope" (1 Thessalonians 4:13). Paul goes on to explain why the Christian has hope even while he is weeping. To begin with, for the Christian, death is sleep; the body goes to sleep, and the soul goes home to God. One day Christ will return and will bring with Him those who have died in Christ and gone on before us; and we shall "ever be with the Lord" (v. 17). When a Christian loved one or friend dies, and we weep, our mourning is certainly not for the loved one but for ourselves. Death is like an amputation, and the closer we are in life the harder it is in death. But our sorrow need not be hopeless, because we have eternal hope in Jesus Christ and in the promises of His Word.

UNNATURAL SORROW

The second kind of sorrow is *unnatural* sorrow. It is unnatural because its effects on our lives are opposite to what God wants us to experience. Godly sorrow heals, but unnatural sorrow makes the wounds deeper and fills the heart with pain. Natural sorrow gradually helps us to put life back together again, but unnatural sorrow tears things apart and keeps them that way. When you sorrow in a natural way, you learn to face and accept reality; but unnatural sorrow isolates you from reality and makes it difficult for you to adjust to the demands of life. I have known people who have grieved themselves into physical affliction and even mental unbalance. True sorrow enables us to experience the comfort of God, but unnatural sorrow blinds us to God's comfort and seems to give us, instead, the condemnation of God—there is a growing feeling of guilt instead of an experience of grace. Natural sorrow enables us to remember the lost loved one and use those memories constructively; but unnatural sorrow turns memories into punishments that destroy the peace and balance that God wants us to have.

Psychologists who have studied bereavement tell us that unnatural sorrow can have many causes. One major cause is selfishness. A self-centered person uses other people—even the closest loved ones—to make his own life safe and pleasant; and if he loses a loved one it upsets his life-style, and it hurts. His tears are more for himself than for the deceased. Fear is another cause of unnatural sorrow—fear of the future, fear of change, perhaps even fear of death itself. Excessive tears and mourning then becomes an invisible armor to protect the person from the hard knocks of life. He is saying, "Don't lay any responsibility on me! Don't demand too much of me! Can't you see I have enough to bear already?"

But perhaps the greatest cause of unnatural grief is guilt: it is our way of atoning for past failures and sins in connection with the deceased. Some people atone for their sins by purchasing expensive, elaborate funerals. I recall one lady who took her life's savings—all that she had—and bought her husband the most expensive casket available. She put her financial future into the grave with him, but it was her way of saying to him, "Dear, I'm sorry for the mean things I said and did while you were sick." I think of another man who visited his wife's grave almost every day for months after her death, no matter what the weather was, not as a sign of love but as a work of atonement. It reminded me of the great Samuel Johnson, who stood in the rain with his head uncovered to atone for a boyish act of disobedience to his father.

King David illustrates this unnatural sorrow caused by guilt. You will recall that David's disobedient son, Absalom, tried to take the kingdom away from him—and almost succeeded. We get the impression that Absalom was a favored, pampered son; certainly he was a vain fellow who was proud of his beauty, especially his hair (2 Samuel 14:25-26). He secretly plotted against his father, drove David from Jerusalem, took over the palace, and then planned to attack David's divided forces and utterly wipe them out. Instead, David won the battle and Absalom was slain, a judgment the young man certainly deserved. Before the battle, David begged his leaders, "Deal gently for my sake with the young man, even with Absalom" (2 Samuel 18:5). When David received the tragic news that Absalom had been slain, he expressed his sorrow in words that have become familiar: "O my son Absalom, my son, my son Absalom! Would God I had died for thee, O Absalom, my son, my son!" (2 Samuel 18:33). While we admire David's love, we question his thinking. Would it have been better for the nation for David to die and for rebellious Absalom to live?

There is no doubt that Absalom's death was part of the payment that David made because of his adultery with Bathsheba. When confronted with the sin of "the rich man" who stole the ewe lamb—a picture of David himself—the king said, "As the Lord liveth, the man that hath done this thing shall surely die: and he shall restore the lamb fourfold, because he did this thing, and because he had no pity" (2 Samuel 12:3-6). David did restore fourfold: the baby died, his daughter Tamar was violated, his son Amnon was slain, and Absalom was slain. Because David temporarily lost control of himself, he temporarily lost the rule over his kingdom. It was a great price to pay for a few moments of pleasure.

But David's mourning over Absalom was not natural. Second Samuel 19 tells us that the soldiers were actually ashamed of their victory because it brought such sorrow to their king! David refused to be comforted. Why? Because he was atoning for his sins. It took the blunt speech of Joab to show the king how selfish he was. "I perceive," said Joab, "that if Absalom had lived, and all we had died this day, then it had pleased thee well" (2 Samuel 19:6). David's abnormal grief had so isolated him from reality that he was unable to live like a king and rule over himself and his people.

The sorrows of life do not *create* problems, they *reveal* them. Absalom's death and David's unnatural mourning revealed to the world that David had not been in control of his own family and that his own sins had found him out. Instead of trying to atone for his sin, David should have trusted God for the forgiveness that he needed. That is what he did when he confessed his sin of adultery, and God graciously forgave him. "For thou desirest not sacrifice; else would I give it: thou delightest not in burnt-offering. The sacrifices of God are a broken spirit: a broken and a contrite heart, O God, thou wilt not despise" (Psalm 51:16-17).

Today we do not bring bulls and goats; we bring excessive tears as our sacrifices. Yet God wants neither one! The comfort of God comes to those who trust the grace of God, not to those who try to earn God's comfort by unnatural sorrow. Even though our sorrows may be caused by our sins, as were David's, we can still confess those sins to the Lord, claim His forgiveness, and experience His comfort. Absalom almost stole the kingdom from David, but David almost lost it by his own foolishness! When you reign in life you have control over your own emotions; when you give way to unnatural sorrow, you get off the throne and lose control of life.

Supernatural Sorrow

But the main thrust of this Beatitude is *supernatural* sorrow. Jesus is talking about repentance for sin, and that is the result of the supernatural working of God in your life. "For godly sorrow worketh repentance to salvation not to be repented of: but the sorrow of the world worketh death" (2 Corinthians 7:10).

This godly sorrow is the logical result of the experience of the first Beatitude: "Blessed are the poor in spirit: for theirs is the kingdom of heaven." When a person sees his spiritual bankruptcy, he can respond in one of four ways. He can deny that his bankruptcy exists and, like the Pharisees, put on a front. But that leads to a life of deception, in which the person uses most of his strength to pretend, so that he has little energy left for living. Second, he can admit his spiritual bankruptcy and try to change things himself. But this is a case of the poor helping the poor! Third, he can admit his need and so despair over it that he gives up completely. This is "the sorrow of the world" that produces death. Judas saw he was a sinner and committed suicide. Peter saw he was a sinner and wept bitterly. That is the difference between the sorrow of the world and the godly sorrow that leads to repentance. The logical thing for a person to do when he sees his own spiritual need is to admit it and then *turn to God for what he needs*. The person who is sincerely poor in spirit will mourn over himself and his sins, and through this mourning he will experience the comfort of God.

We must distinguish, however, between repentance and remorse and regret. When my consciousness of sin rests only in my mind, then it is regret. When it affects my mind and my heart, it is remorse, and remorse is a dangerous thing. But when my concern over my sin brings me to the place where I am willing to turn from it and obey God—when my concern affects my *will* as well as my mind and my heart—then I have experienced true repentance.

You may remember the story about the Sunday school teacher who asked a pupil to define repentance, and the boy replied: "Repentance means sorrow for sin." "That's right!" said the teacher. But then a little girl spoke up: "Excuse me, but it means being sorry enough to quit!" She knew that repentance involves not only a change in feeling and thinking but also a change of the *will*. If a person truly changes his mind about sin he will act differently.

The prodigal son (Luke 15) illustrates the truth perfectly; his mind, heart, and will were all involved in his repentance. His mind told him that his father's servants were better off than he was; his heart made him sick of his situation—"I perish with hunger!"—and his will motivated him to arise and go to his father. Had he sat there in the pigpen thinking how foolish he had been, it would have been regret. Had he thought about his sins and hated himself for committing them, it would have been remorse. When he said, "I will arise and go!"—and he arose and went—that was repentance. His sorrow was a godly sorrow that motivated him to return home and experience forgiveness.

About what are we supposed to repent? Obviously, we should repent of our sins. "For I will declare my iniquity; I will be sorry for my sin" (Psalm 38:18). We must be careful that it is *sin* over which we sorrow and not the painful consequences of sin or the fact that we have been caught. Too many people fail to see the difference. When the sinner repents of his sins and puts his faith in Jesus Christ, then he is saved. This was Paul's message: "repentance toward God, and faith toward our Lord Jesus Christ" (Acts 20:21).

Does God expect His own children to repent? I believe He does. Paul commended the believers at Corinth because they received his letter and "sorrowed to repentance" (2 Corinthians 7:9). On the other hand, Paul warned that same church that he would come and discipline those who had not repented, and certainly he was talking about professed Christians (2 Corinthians 12:21). In His last message to the church, our Lord commands His people to repent (Revelation 2:5, 16; 3:3, 19).

We must beware of an easy and comfortable dealing with our sins. It was this surface dealing with sin that cost King Saul his crown. The record is in 1 Samuel 15. First, Saul lied about his sin: "I have performed the commandment of the Lord" (v. 13). Then, he made an excuse instead of a confession: it was "the people" who had disobeyed God, not Saul! Finally, Saul used religion to defend sin! He said he would use the animals that were spared as sacrifices for the Lord! Even after Samuel exposed Saul's wickedness, the king persisted in defending himself and blaming the people (vv. 20-21). And when King Saul finally said, "I have sinned" (v. 30), he still qualified his confession with a condition: "Yet honor me now, I pray thee, before the elders of my people, and before

Israel" (v. 30). He was more concerned about his reputation than his character, what men thought rather than what God thought.

From that point on, Saul began to lose his kingdom, and David began to gain his kingdom. It was David, not Saul, who defeated Goliath (1 Samuel 17). David slew tens of thousands of the enemy, whereas Saul slew only thousands (1 Samuel 18:7). Saul began to fear and suspect; he tried to kill David; he even turned against Jonathan, his own son. God departed from Saul, and the record closes with King Saul turning to Satan for help, inquiring of a witch (1 Samuel 28), and then dying in shame on the field of battle. Nothing leads to defeat in the Christian life like a surface dealing with sin.

This does not mean that the disobedient believer must wallow in self-reproach and condemnation, because even that attitude could be sinful. Paul told the Corinthians to forgive the man who had been guilty of sin, "lest perhaps such a one should be swallowed up with overmuch sorrow" (2 Corinthians 2:7). Why? "Lest Satan should get an advantage of us" (2 Corinthians 2:11). Satan is the "accuser of the brethren" (Revelation 12:10); he likes nothing better than to remind the saints of their sins and make them miserable to the point of giving up.

There are two extremes to avoid when it comes to dealing with our sins: being too easy on ourselves and being too hard on ourselves. Either extreme will cost us the enjoyment of our kingdom. King Saul was too easy on his sins, and he lost the crown; and David was too hard on himself at the death of Absalom, and he almost lost the crown.

As Christians we must repent of our sins. That means more than admitting them and trying to explain or excuse them. It means admitting them, looking upon them the way God does, abhorring them, and turning from them.

"A broken and a contrite heart, O God, thou wilt not despise" (Psalm 51:17). Simply quoting 1 John 1:9 in a glib manner is not true repentance. That promise is not an excuse for sin; it is an encouragement to believers who want to get rid of sin. "If we confess our sins, he is faithful and just to forgive us our sins, and to cleanse us from all unrighteousness." That word *confess* literally means "to say the same thing." If I am to be forgiven, I must agree with God's verdict about my sins. King Saul said, "I have sinned" and then proceeded to argue with the prophet and make excuses. King David said, "I have sinned," and the prophet said to him, "The Lord also hath put away thy sin; thou shalt not die" (2 Samuel 12:13).

It is necessary for us to repent of our sins, but that is only the beginning. Anyone can mourn over his sins, but not too many people mourn over the fact that they are sinners. We should show sorrow not only for what we do but for what we are. This kind of sorrow seems strange to the superficial Christian; but it was not strange to godly men and women of the Bible and the saints of church history. "Behold, I was shapen in iniquity; and in sin did my mother conceive me" (Psalm 51:5) was not David's excuse for his disobedience. It was his expression of a deeper repentance. "I am not only sorry for what I did, but I am also sorry for what I am." As you read Psalm 51, you realize that David was confessing the fact that his very being was polluted by sin. His "inward parts" were defiled (v. 6), his ears no longer heard joy (v. 8), his heart was dirty, and his spirit needed renewal (v. 10)—even his tongue and his lips were paralyzed by sin (vv. 14-15)! His eyes saw nothing but sin: "my sin is ever before me" (v. 3). Here is a man who repented of his sins—but not in a superficial way: he exposed every part of his being to the searchlight of God.

But this mourning goes even deeper. We repent not only of what we do and what we are, but we also mourn over what sin does in this world. Jeremiah wept over the sins of his people. Jesus wept over the sins of Jerusalem. Paul wept as he ministered in the churches. All of creation is groaning because of sin, and the believer joins in that groaning (Romans 8:22-23). Although we thank God that He gives to us in this world "richly all things to enjoy" (1 Timothy 6:17), we also weep because our Father's world has been so polluted and plundered by sin. The present crisis in ecology is but a symptom of that deeper crisis. Many people weep over the loss of precious resources and the marring of irreplaceable beauty, but few weep over the godless rebellion in man's heart that has caused this crisis.

We not only mourn over sin in our lives and in the world God made, but we also mourn over sin in the lives of others. When a member of the church at Corinth was living in shameless incest, the church members should have mourned; but instead they boasted of their open-mindedness (1 Corinthians 5)! "Ye are puffed up, and have not rather mourned," Paul scolded (v. 2). The Greek word translated "mourned" means "to mourn as for the dead." If the believers at Corinth had truly mourned because of that sin, they would have lovingly dealt with the offender and brought him to a place of repentance. "Brethren, if a man be overtaken in a fault, ye which are spiritual restore such an one in the spirit of meekness" (Galatians 6:1).

The Christian who is able to deal with sin in his own life can be trusted to deal with sin in the lives of others. He will be neither too easy nor too hard. It is often the case that those who are too easy on themselves will be hard on others. Saul excused himself for disobeying God, yet he threatened to kill his son Jonathan for disobeying his (Saul's) own foolish commandment (1 Samuel 14:24-25). David was excessively hard on himself and yet too easy on Absalom. Maintaining a balance in dealing with sin—our own and others'—requires the wisdom of God and the leading of His Spirit. Satan welcomes either extreme. If we are too easy in dealing with sin, the matter is not settled to the glory of God; if we are too hard, it could result in "overmuch sorrow" and defeat.

It may seem strange, but this mourning over sin can go even deeper. We mourn over what we do, what we are, and what sin has wrought in this world and in the lives of others; but we also mourn over our mourning. This may sound neurotic, but it is not. As we grow in grace, we realize more and more how inadequate we are to face God and deal with our sins. Jeremiah was not satisfied with his mourning. "Oh that my head were waters, and mine eyes a fountain of tears, that I might weep day and night for the slain of the daughter of my people!" (Jeremiah 9:1). "For these things I weep; mine eye, mine eye runneth down with water" (Lamentations 1:16). As one reads his Lamentations, one realizes how deeply his heart was moved because of sin; and the sin was not even his own!

When you and I learn how to mourn, then we will have a deeper understanding of the sinfulness of sin and the graciousness of God.

SPIRITUAL COMFORT

Christ promises comfort to those who mourn, but what kind of comfort is it? You can be sure that it is far deeper than sympathy, the drying of the tears and the enfolding of the child in the arms of love. Our English word *comfort* comes from two Latin words that mean "with strength" (The words *fortify* and *fortress* carry the same meaning.) We are prone to confuse *comfort* and *sympathy*, but they are not identical. To sympathize means "to feel with," whereas to comfort means "to encourage, to give strength." Our mourning puts us in touch with the eternal resources of God, and the result is God's comfort. "In the day when I cried thou answeredst me, and strengthenedst me with strength in my soul" (Psalm 138:3).

Our God is the "God of all comfort" (2 Corinthians 1:3). His attitude toward us is not one of hostility, but one of love and encouragement. He is not against us; He is *for* us. This is one of the emphases in Romans 8. The Holy Spirit makes intercession for us (v. 26). God the Father delivered up His Son for us (v. 32). God the Son is making intercession for us (v. 34). No wonder Paul cried, "If God be for us, who can be against us?" (v. 31). " 'For I know the plans that I have for you,' declares the Lord, 'plans for welfare and not for calamity to give you a future and a hope' " (Jeremiah 29:11, NASB*). Our comfort and encouragement is God Himself. "But David encouraged himself in the Lord his God" (1 Samuel 30:6). How different from King Saul, who refused to mourn over his sin. "Then Saul fell straightway all along on the earth, and was sore afraid" (1 Samuel 28:20).

We have also the comfort of the Scriptures. "For whatsoever things were written aforetime were written for our learning, that we through patience and comfort of the scriptures might have hope. Now the God of patience and consolation grant you to be like-minded toward one another according to Christ Jesus" (Romans 15:4-5). The same Word that reveals our sins also reveals the grace and forgiveness of God. Nathan said to David, "Thou art the man!" (2 Samuel 12:7). But he also said, "The Lord also hath put away thy sin" (v. 13). The sinful woman mourned at Jesus' feet, and He said to her, "Thy sins are forgiven. . . . Thy faith hath saved thee; go in peace" (Luke 7:48, 50). To the woman taken in the act of adultery He said, "Neither do I condemn thee: go, and sin no more" (John 8:11).

New American Standard Bible.

God also gives us the comfort of the Holy Spirit, for the Spirit is the Comforter (John 14:16). He is the great Encourager, the One who puts strength in our souls. In the Scriptures we have the *objective* source of comfort; and in the Spirit within, we have the *subjective* source of comfort. The same Spirit who wrote the Word lives in our hearts, and He opens up the Scriptures so that His comfort comes into our lives. Only those who have experienced the comforting ministry of the Holy Spirit can understand this holy experience.

Finally, God comforts us through His people. Often the Holy Spirit uses another Christian to bring us the encouragement that we need. God comforted Paul by the coming of Titus (2 Corinthians 7:6), and Titus comforted Paul by reporting that the problems in the church were being solved. In fact, one reason we as Christians go through difficulties is so that we might be able to experience the comfort of God and then share that comfort with others. God "comforteth us in all our tribulation, that we may be able to comfort them which are in any trouble, by the comfort wherewith we ourselves are comforted of God" (2 Corinthians 1:4). This does not mean that we must experience exactly the same trials to be of encouragement to others, because God's comfort enables us to encourage those who are in "any trouble." God's comfort is not a luxury for us to hoard; it is a necessity that we must share. "Bear ye one another's burdens, and so fulfill the law of Christ" (Galatians 6:2).

THE MAN OF SORROWS

Our Lord was a "man of sorrows, and acquainted with grief" (Isaiah 53:3). He knew what it was to mourn, not over His own sins, of course, because He had no sin (2 Corinthians 5:21), but over the sins of the world and the havoc sin wrought in the world. He wept at the tomb of

Lazarus, even though He knew He would raise Lazarus from the dead. In the garden Jesus wept "with strong crying and tears" (Hebrews 5:7) as He faced the cross, knowing that the eternal sorrow for sin would come upon Him there. What a paradox that He should suffer such great sorrow, at the same time looking to "the joy that was set before him" (Hebrews 12:2).

That Jesus Christ was the Man of Sorrows suggests that, as we experience true mourning for sin, we become more like Christ. It is significant that the people believed that Jesus was Jeremiah returned from the grave (Matthew 16:14), because Jeremiah, too, was a man of sorrows and acquainted with grief. "Is it nothing to you, all ye that pass by? Behold, and see if there be any sorrow like unto my sorrow" (Lamentations 1:12). Of course, we must not major in mourning; there is also the "joy of the Lord," which is our strength (Nehemiah 8:10). But as we pray, we see ourselves (as did Abraham) "but dust and ashes" (Genesis 18:27). As we see God's blessing, we confess with Peter: "Depart from me; for I am a sinful man, O Lord" (Luke 5:8). There is always new mourning, and there is always new comfort; and this process makes us more like the Master.

The tears of the believer work *for* him and are an investment in future joys. Not all of our comfort will be given today. "Weeping may endure for a night, but joy cometh in the morning" (Psalm 30:5). "They that sow in tears shall reap in joy" (Psalm 126:5). "God shall wipe away all tears from their eyes" (Revelation 21:4). Psalm 56:8 teaches us that none of our tears will go unnoticed by God: "Put thou my tears into thy bottle: are they not in thy book?" If God sees the sparrow fall, will He not also see our tears fall? Heaven will be a place of no tears, but hell will be a place of nothing but tears. It was Jesus who said, "There shall be weeping and gnashing of teeth" (Matthew 8:12).

There is one way that the believer will never become like the Man of Sorrows: He never wept for Himself; He always wept for others. He said to the sympathetic women of Jerusalem, "Weep not for me, but weep for yourselves, and for your children" (Luke 23:28). Until we see Him in glory and become like Him, we will have to weep for ourselves. "Not as though I had already attained, either were already perfect" (Philippians 3:12). But as we weep, we can be sure of His promise: "Blessed are they that mourn: for they shall be comforted."

Blessed are the meek: for they shall inherit the earth.
(Matthew 5:5)

Take my yoke upon you, and learn of me; for I am meek and lowly in heart: and ye shall find rest unto your souls.
(Matthew 11:29)

Now the man Moses was very meek, above all the men which were upon the face of the earth.
(Numbers 12:3)

The fruit of the Spirit is . . . meekness.
(Galatians 5:22-23)

With all lowliness and meekness, with longsuffering, forbearing one another in love.
(Ephesians 4:2)

Receive with meekness the engrafted word.
(James 1:21)

5

The Meek

MEEKNESS IS NOT WEAKNESS

Let's begin with the meaning of meekness. Most people have the idea that meekness is weakness. We live in a world that worships power and rejects any evidence of weakness; perhaps this explains why many successful people will have little or nothing to do with the Christian faith. They have heard about "Gentle Jesus, meek and mild," and they want nothing to do with Him. The ladder of success in today's world is climbed with heavy steps; there is no place for timidity.

But meekness is not weakness or timidity. Meekness is power under control. Certainly nobody could accuse Moses of being a weak, timid man; yet God identified him as the meekest man on the face of the earth. Jesus was the most courageous man ever to walk among men, and yet He said, "I am meek and lowly in heart" (Matthew 11:29). Both Moses and Jesus faced difficult, dangerous situations and came through victoriously because they exercised power under control.

God has given us the ability to become angry. Nowhere does the Bible honor the spineless person who is unable (or unwilling) to exercise the right kind of anger. "Be ye angry, and sin not" (Ephesians 4:26). There is a sinless anger, such as when Moses came down from Mount Sinai and saw his people reveling in sin or when Jesus strode into the Temple and majestically cleansed His Father's house. There is a godless anger that destroys, but there is a godly anger that builds up. Two verses from Proverbs explain the difference: "He that is slow to anger is better than the mighty; and he that ruleth his spirit than he that taketh a city" (Proverbs 16:32). That is power under control. "He that hath no rule over his own spirit is like a city that is broken down, and without walls" (Proverbs 25:28). That is power out of control.

Someone has said, "Temper is such a wonderful thing that it's a shame to lose it!" We temper steel to make it stronger. The person who loses his temper loses control of himself and stops living like a king. A successful businessman, Roger Babson, once said, "The best administrator is the governor of his temper."

"Anyone can become angry," wrote Aristotle in his *Nicomachean Ethics.* "That is easy. But to be angry with the right person, to the right degree, at the right time, for the right purpose, and in the right way—this is not easy." What the great philosopher was talking about was meekness—power under control. Anger is power, just as fire is power. (We sometimes say, "His anger flared up!") When fire is under control, it is our servant and accomplishes great things for us; but when fire is out of control, it becomes our master, and the result is destruction. So it is with anger.

"There is nothing wrong with losing my temper," a lady once told evangelist Billy Sunday. "I blow up, and then it's over with."

"So does a shotgun," the evangelist replied, "but look at the damage that's left behind."

The Greek word that is translated "meekness" was a familiar word to the people in Jesus' day. It was used to describe a soothing medicine. A patient who is wrestling with a fever is given medication by his doctor to quiet him down and relieve the burning so that he can sleep. The word also was used by sailors to describe a gentle breeze. Have you ever been exhausted on a hot day and then felt a cooling breeze blow on your body? It is refreshing. But doctors and sailors were not the only ones to use that word, because farmers used it, too. It was used to describe a colt that has been broken. Every colt has to be broken, or it cannot fulfill its function on the farm. Somebody has to break the colt so that its power can be channeled into constructive work.

Look at these three illustrations: medicine, wind, and a colt. What do they all have in common? Power! Medicine has power to work in the body to calm nerves, kill germs, strengthen organs, and promote healing. The wind also has power. In 1965 "Hurricane Betsy" did more than a billion dollars' worth of damage and cost insurance companies $750 million in claims. That is power! If you have ever watched a cowboy on a bucking bronco, you know that a horse is a powerful animal. But the medicine, wind, and horse must keep their power under control, otherwise they will do damage. The proper dosage of medicine can promote healing, but an overdose may kill. A summer breeze is a delightful thing, but a hurricane only destroys. A broken horse can give both work and pleasure to his master, but a horse out of control is dangerous. All of these have power, and when that power is under control it is called meekness.

MEET THE MEEK

Perhaps the best way to understand meekness is to see it at work in the lives of people like ourselves.

When Abraham left Ur of the Chaldees, he took his nephew Lot with him, and it was not long before there was a family disagreement. "There was a strife between the herdmen of Abraham's cattle and the herdmen of Lot's cattle" (Genesis 13:7). If you were Abraham, what would you have done? Certainly Abraham had the authority to tell Lot to pack up and get moving! After all, Abraham was God's chosen servant; he was even called "the friend of God." It was Abraham whom God called and with whom God had made His covenant; Lot was simply a tagalong. Abraham had power over Lot, but he kept that power under control. He exercised meekness.

> Abram said unto Lot, Let there be no strife, I pray thee, between me and thee, and between my herdmen and thy herdmen; for we be brethren. Is not the whole land before thee? separate thyself, I pray thee, from me: if thou wilt take the left hand, then I will go to the right; or if thou depart to the right hand, then I will go to the left. (Genesis 13:8-9)

Had Abraham been like most of us, he would have said, "I am the elder of this clan, and I get first choice!" To many people, that kind of an attitude would have been "exercising leadership." To God, it would have been committing sin. Abraham had power, but his power was under control, and he gave Lot first choice. "In honor preferring one another" (Romans 12:10). "Let each esteem others more important than themselves" (Philippians 2:3, literal translation). Because Abraham was surrendered to God, he was not afraid to submit to Lot. Abraham knew that his own inheritance was secure in the Lord and that no decision on the part of his nephew could ever rob him of anything that God had for him. Abraham had power, but his power was under control; so God kept His promise and enabled Abraham to "inherit the earth."

Joseph is another vivid illustration of meekness. Mistreated by his brothers, Joseph was sold into Egypt as a slave. Lied about by his master's wife, he was put into prison. But one day, Joseph was elevated to become the prime minister of Egypt. He had the power to revenge himself on his master's wife, but there is no record that he ever did. And then his brothers showed up, begging for food, and although Joseph could have refused them or punished them, he did not. To be sure, he dealt with them so that they confessed their sins and gave evidence of true repentance; but in the end Joseph refused to hurt them. He had power over them, but he kept his power under control.

Remember: meekness does not show itself when we are wrong, but when we are right. Meekness is not the shamefaced boy who is caught with his hand in the cookie jar. Meekness is not embarrassment when I am caught doing something wrong. Meekness is power under control. It reveals itself when I am right and when I have the power to hurt someone who is wrong.

I think of David as another illustration of meekness. David's greatest victories were not with his hands, but with his heart. In 1 Samuel 24, Saul blundered into the cave where David and his men were hiding, and then went to sleep. With one flashing stroke of his sword, David could have killed Saul and taken the throne. In fact, some of David's men urged him to do just that, putting an end to the man who was chasing them and seeking their lives. Instead of cutting off Saul's head, David quietly cut off the skirt of Saul's robe; and even that action made him feel guilty. David had the power to kill Saul, but he kept his power under control.

There was another episode in David's life that reveals his meekness in an even greater measure. It is recorded in 2 Samuel 16. David's son Absalom took over the kingdom and forced his father to flee into the wilderness. During that difficult time, one of Saul's men, Shimei, cursed David and threw stones at him. Abishai, David's nephew, said to the king, "Let me go over, I pray thee, and take off his head" (v. 9). That would have been a reasonable thing to do in that day, but David would not permit it. His only answer was, "Let him alone, and let him curse; for the Lord hath bidden him" (v. 11). That is power under control.

You can be sure that Saul would have killed David had he caught him in the cave; and no doubt Saul would have killed Shimei as well. The difference between those two kings is not that one had power and the other did not—for both had power. The difference is that David's power was under control. He was a meek man. David used his authority to build up people; Saul used people to build up his authority. At one time, Saul was going to kill his own son for a trivial matter, just to show the people how powerful he was (1 Samuel 14:36-45). David was willing to die for his own son, even though Absalom was a rebel (2 Samuel 18:33).

Of course, the greatest example of meekness is the Lord Jesus Christ. "He is brought as a lamb to the slaughter, and as a sheep before her shearers is dumb, so he openeth not his mouth" (Isaiah 53:7). "Who, when he was reviled, reviled not again; when he suffered, he threatened not; but committed himself to him that judgeth righteously" (1 Peter 2:23). It took more power for Jesus to submit than for Peter to draw out his sword and fight. Peter's action was natural; what our Lord did was supernatural. Jesus exercised power under control. He could have summoned legions of angels, but instead he "became obedient unto death, even the death of the cross" (Philippians 2:8).

How can you and I tell whether or not we are meek?

Perhaps the simplest answer is a question: are we exercising self-control? Is our power under control? We have physical power, mental power, emotional power, even spiritual power. Are we keeping all of this power under control?

But I believe that the best test of meekness is found in the word *attitude*. For example, what is our attitude toward the circumstances of life? When Jesus said, "Blessed are the meek, for they shall inherit the earth," He was quoting from Psalm 37:11: "But the meek shall inherit the earth; and shall delight themselves in the abundance of peace." When you read Psalm 37, you discover that the writer was going through a great deal of trouble. Evil unbelievers were trying to cut him down. They were slandering him and trying to ruin his reputation. In fact, they were plotting against him and trying to take his life! Perhaps you and I have never had our lives threatened, but we have experienced difficult circumstances. How do we respond to them? What is our attitude toward the difficulties of life?

Too many people respond—or react—to the difficulties of life by fretting. "Fret not thyself!" says the opening verse of Psalm 37, and it is repeated in verse 8: "Cease from anger, and forsake wrath: fret not thyself in any wise to do evil." The normal thing to do when people attack you is to get angry, fret over it, and fight back; but this is not the spiritual thing to do. The meek man submits himself *and his enemy* to God and lets Him handle the problem. Look at the admonitions in Psalm 37: "Trust in the Lord. . . . Delight thyself also in the Lord. . . . Rest in the

Lord, and wait patiently for him. . . . Cease from anger.
. . . Depart from evil, and do good" (vv. 3-4, 7-8, 27). The
meek man centers his attention and his affection on *the
Lord*, not on himself or his adversary. When you find
yourself fretting because of people or circumstances, you
can be sure that you have lost your meekness.

Another test of meekness is one's attitude toward
God's Word. James 1:19 commands us to be "swift to
hear, slow to speak, slow to wrath." James 1:21 commands us to "receive with meekness the engrafted [im-
parted] word." James wrote his letter to a group of Christians who were at war with each other! "From whence
come wars and fightings among you?" (4:1). One reason
for their division was a stubborn attitude toward God's
Word. Instead of receiving God's Word with meekness
—like planting seed in soft soil—they were arguing and
becoming angry. They were not "slow to speak, slow to
wrath." The meek Christian submits to the Word of God
and receives it gladly into a prepared heart.

Again we see the contrast between Saul and David.
When Samuel gave Saul God's message, the king argued
with it and tried to excuse himself. He blamed the people—and he even blamed Samuel! "Because I saw that
the people were scattered from me, and that thou camest
not within the days appointed, and that the Philistines
gathered themselves together" (1 Samuel 13:11). Later,
God gave Saul another chance to live like a king, and
again he failed. Instead of slaying the enemy as he was
commanded (1 Samuel 15), he kept the best for himself
and then blamed the people! "But the people took of the
spoil . . . to sacrifice unto the Lord thy God in Gilgal" (v.
21). Saul was not a meek man; he refused to submit to the
Word of God.

But David submitted and "received with meekness
the engrafted word." David's chaplain, Nathan, took his
life in his hands when he confronted the king with his

adultery and murder (2 Samuel 12), for David was a back-slidden man and could have ordered the prophet to be killed. Nathan told the touching story about the one little ewe lamb that the rich man stole from the poor man, "and David's anger was greatly kindled against the man" (v. 5). Bravely, Nathan said, "Thou art the man"—and waited. Would David's anger be kindled against his prophet? No, because David was a meek man, and he received God's Word without arguing, making excuses, or defending himself. "I have sinned against the Lord!" (v. 13). He was a man after God's own heart.

The third test of meekness is one's attitude toward a brother who sins. Do I receive the news gleefully and start to spread it? Am I pleased that he has sinned, because his fall makes my walk look better? "Brethren, if a man be overtaken in a fault, ye which are spiritual, restore such a one in the spirit of meekness; considering thyself, lest thou also be tempted" (Galatians 6:1). When a Christian brother has fallen into sin, I have the power to hurt him; but meekness is power under control. I also have the power to help him. "Restore such an one." That word *restore* was used by doctors in Paul's day; it means "to set a broken bone." When a Christian falls into sin, it affects the Body of Christ the way a broken bone affects your physical body: it must be restored. My first response to a brother's sin ought to be sorrow and pity and then a desire to help him get back into fellowship with God. Shimei threw stones at David when David was at his weakest physically and politically; yet David proved himself to be the stronger man spiritually. Later, when David's throne was restored, Shimei came to beg forgiveness, and David forgave him. He restored him in a spirit of meekness (2 Samuel 19:16-23).

A broken bone is painful, and setting it can be even more painful than the break itself. A doctor does not use a crowbar and a pipe wrench to set a broken bone; he uses power under control. That is meekness.

A fourth test of meekness is one's attitude toward division in the church. "I therefore, the prisoner of the Lord, beseech you that ye walk worthy of the vocation [calling] wherewith ye are called, with all lowliness and meekness, with longsuffering, forbearing one another in love; endeavouring to keep the unity of the Spirit in the bond of peace" (Ephesians 4:1-3). There are people in every church who are always wanting to take sides and divide God's people.

When I was a boy in the junior department of Sunday school, I remember hearing a teacher say, "Well, there's a business meeting this week, and I'm going to be there loaded for bear!" The next Sunday a number of people were missing from the services, and I discovered that the "hunter" had shot off his mouth, and there had been a church split.

The Christian who exercises meekness is not interested in taking sides; he is interested in "being diligent to preserve the unity of the Spirit in the bond of peace" (Ephesians 4:3, NASB). He follows the example of Abraham: "Let there be no strife, I pray thee, between me and thee . . . for we be brethren" (Genesis 13:8).

The fifth test of meekness in our lives concerns our attitude toward those people who disagree with us. "The servant of the Lord must not strive; but be gentle unto all men, apt to teach, patient, in meekness instructing those that oppose themselves; if God peradventure will give them repentance to the acknowledging of the truth" (2 Timothy 2:24-25). It is possible to win arguments and lose friends—and souls!

The poet Oliver Goldsmith said of Samuel Johnson, England's "czar of literature": "There is no arguing with Johnson, for if his pistol misses fire, he knocks you down with the butt end of it!" Some Christians are like that.

"Watch out for So-and-so," a friend warned me. "He uses a cannon to kill a mosquito!" It is a mark of meekness—and maturity—when we realize that good people disagree and that God can bless people with whom we disagree. Even the person who opposes the Word of God has a better chance of being convinced if we have a meek and gentle spirit. I like J. W. C. Wand's translation of this passage: "The Lord's servant must not quarrel, but be gentle to all, good at teaching, slow to take offense, one who can reduce his opponents by the mildness of his manners."

Finally, what is my attitude toward the unsaved? "But sanctify the Lord God in your hearts: and be ready always to give an answer to every man that asketh you a reason of the hope that is in you with meekness and fear" (1 Peter 3:15). Peter is warning against arguing with lost souls and using the Bible as a club to beat them down. He is telling us to be witnesses and not prosecuting attorneys! Too often we use high-pressure salesmanship methods in our zeal to win souls, but that is power out of control. Jesus could have overpowered Nicodemus or crushed the woman of Samaria, but instead He patiently led them into the truth of the Word of God.

MEEKNESS GROWS IN TRIALS

How can the believer go about cultivating this grace of meekness? Galatians 5:23 tells us that meekness is not something that we manufacture; it is part of the "fruit of the Spirit." Fruit is not manufactured; fruit must be cultivated. There was a time when Moses, the meekest man on earth, became angry at an enemy and killed him. God had to put Moses on the backside of the desert for forty years, taking care of his father-in-law's sheep, in order to prepare him for his ministry. Alone in the desert, caring for the meekest of animals, Moses began to learn meekness. He was the adopted son of Pharaoh's daughter, educated in all the wisdom of Egypt, and yet he became a shepherd.

We cultivate meekness in the difficult experiences of life.

Think of what Moses had to endure as he led the people of Israel. No sooner was the nation delivered from Egypt than the people began to complain; and they complained for the next forty years until that generation died. They complained about the way God led them and about the way He fed them. They rebelled against Moses' authority. They tried to organize a party to return to Egypt. When Moses finally brought them to the border of the Promised Land, they refused to go in! All of his sacrifice and work was for nothing! No, it was not for nothing; for Moses was "growing in grace" and cultivating the wonderful grace of meekness. Moses had always had power, but it was not under control. It was in the school of hard knocks that he learned to be meek.

King Saul never learned meekness because he always tried to scheme his way out of the difficulties of life. Instead of trials' bringing out the best in him, they brought out his worst. And he always had an excuse ready whenever Samuel showed up. "An excuse," said Billy Sunday, "is the skin of a reason, stuffed with a lie." People who are good at excuses are rarely good at anything else. But David profited from the trials of life and, in spite of his failures (and we all have them), learned how to be meek. Saul tried to use his own authority to make himself great, but David said to God, "Thy gentleness hath made me great" (Psalm 18:35). As David reviewed the trials of his life, he looked back and saw how gentle God had been. Anybody can submit to harshness, but it takes a great man to submit to gentleness. It takes a man whose heart is gentle and whose attitude is that of meekness.

The Saul of the Old Testament never learned meekness, but the Saul of the New Testament did. When Paul the apostle was Saul of Tarsus, he possessed great power. And he used that power to persecute and even to kill. "It is hard for you to kick against the goads," Jesus said to him (Acts 26:14, NASB), suggesting that Saul was like a wild animal that had never been broken. But God broke him, and a spirit of meekness came into his life.

As a Christian and an apostle, Paul had more power and authority than ever before; but he used that power for the good of others and the glory of God. He had learned meekness. The situation in the Corinthian church, for example, was enough to test the patience of Job; yet when you read Paul's Corinthian letters you see power under control. "What will ye?" he asks in 1 Corinthians 4:21. "Shall I come unto you with a rod, or in love, and in the spirit of meekness?" In his second letter he beseeches them "by the meekness and gentleness of Christ" (10:1). To the believers in Galatia, Ephesus, and Colosse, Paul urged the cultivation of meekness; and when he wrote to the pastors—Timothy and Titus—he reminded them to show meekness. Like Elijah on Mount Horeb, Paul had learned that God was not in the wind or the earthquake or the fire, but in "the still, small voice." That is power under control.

You and I must make the choice: Will we submit in the difficulties of life and cultivate meekness, or will we rebel and produce hardness? The fruit of the Spirit is meekness, but it takes time for the fruit to grow; and the fruit grows best in the storms of life.

The Meek Are Enriched

From the world's point of view, meekness is the first step toward failure. Unless you toot your own horn, wave your own flag, and promote your own goals, you will never get anywhere in today's competitive world. Centuries ago, the Athenian statesman Pericles described the situation perfectly when he said, "Fishes in the sea, . . . as men do a-land; the great ones eat up the little ones."

But from the divine point of view, self-promotion is the fastest way to failure. "When thou wast little in thine own sight," Samuel said to King Saul, "wast thou not made the head of the tribes of Israel, and the Lord anointed thee king over Israel?" (1 Samuel 15:17). When Saul was little, God made him great; but when Saul made himself great, God made him nothing. Saul lost his crown.

But David showed a spirit of meekness, so God gave him the crown. "The Spirit of the Lord came upon David . . . but the Spirit of the Lord departed from Saul" (1 Samuel 16:13-14). Because David submitted himself to God, he grew in the trials of life and was prepared by God to sit on the throne and rule Israel. Both David and Jesus, the Son of David, had to suffer and be rejected before they reigned; the same pattern is duplicated in our lives. We reign in life by resigning our lives. "For whosoever will save his life shall lose it, and whosoever will lose his life for my sake shall find it" (Matthew 16:25).

"Blessed are the meek: for they shall inherit the earth." What does that mean? Does it mean that meek people are prosperous in this world's goods? Apparently not, because Jesus was meek and possessed little of this world's goods. Does it mean that meek people escape the difficulties of life? I don't believe so, because Moses was meek and yet he faced one difficulty after another. To answer the question we must go back to Psalm 37, where the original statement is found.

The conflict in this psalm is between the righteous and the wicked. (Note the repetition of "the wicked" in verses 10, 12, 14, 20-21, 28, 32, 34-35, 38, and 40.) It appears that the wicked are winning and the righteous are losing. James Russell Lowell phrased it, "Truth forever on the scaffold, wrong forever on the throne."

What can the righteous do in such a dangerous and difficult situation? Fret? No. God said, "Fret not thyself because of evil-doers" (v. 1). Fight? No. The Lord stands by to protect the righteous and fight their battle for them. "But the salvation of the righteous is of the Lord: he is their strength in the time of trouble" (v. 39).

Then what should the righteous do? *Meekly submit to God's will* by trusting in the Lord (v. 3), delighting in the Lord (v. 4), committing their way unto the Lord (v. 5), and resting in the Lord (v. 7). The result is that they will "inherit the earth," which simply means that they do not have to be afraid of anybody or anything because God is in control of them and their circumstances. To "inherit the earth" means to reign as king over yourself and your circumstances through the power of the Holy Spirit. "Yet a little while, and the wicked shall not be: yea, thou shalt diligently consider his place, and it shall not be. But the meek shall inherit the earth; and shall delight themselves in the abundance of peace" (vv. 10-11).

When you are meek, you seek nothing for yourself; and when you seek nothing for yourself, God gives you all things. Saul's self-seeking cost him his crown; but David's submission gave him the kingdom. Something else is true: meekness means power under control, and when you can control yourself, everything belongs to you! If you can reign in peace over the kingdom within you, then God will give you all you need in the kingdom without.

The saddest event in David's life, his sin with Bathsheba, helps to illustrate this principle. Second Samuel 11:1 says, "At the time when kings go forth to battle. . . . David tarried still at Jerusalem." He was not living like a king! Not only had he taken off his armor, but he had also taken off his crown. The sad result is recorded in the rest of the chapter: adultery, deceit, murder, sin covered and not confessed. About a year later, Nathan rebuked

David for his sins and reminded the king of how much God had given him. "I gave thee thy master's house, and thy master's wives into thy bosom, and gave thee the house of Israel and of Judah; and if that had been too little, I would moreover have given unto thee such and such things" (2 Samuel 12:8). God was saying through Nathan, "David, when you were meek, I gave you blessing after blessing. But when you became proud and disobeyed My word, you started to lose. It is the meek who inherit, not the proud. If you had remained meek before Me, I would have given you all that you needed and desired and more. But now I cannot do it."

The meek person owns everything because he is submitted to the God who made everything and controls everything—God is his Father. "For all things are yours; whether Paul, or Apollos, or Cephas, or the world, or life, or death, or things present, or things to come; all are yours; and ye are Christ's; and Christ is God's" (1 Corinthians 3:21-23). "As having nothing, and yet possessing all things" (2 Corinthians 6:10).

Again, our Lord Jesus Christ is the perfect illustration of this truth. Because He was "meek and lowly in heart," He never worried about the people or the circumstances in the world. You never find Him fretting. Often you find the disciples fretting and even fearing, but never Jesus. He never fretted about the storms, because He knew His Father was in control. In fact, He slept in the storm! He never fretted about food. The disciples asked, "Where can we find enough bread to feed this hungry crowd?" (John 6:5, paraphrased). But Jesus was not worried, because He knew His Father could provide all the bread they needed and more. When the soldiers came to arrest Him, Jesus willingly submitted, because He knew His Father was in control. "The cup which my Father hath given me, shall I not drink it?" (John 18:11).

Those who cannot control themselves are never satisfied. There is a restlessness in their hearts that robs them of the joys that are found in the blessings of God. "Thou hast made us for Thyself," said Augustine, "and our hearts are restless until they rest in Thee." "Rest in the Lord," commands Psalm 37:7, and verse 11 promises, "The meek shall inherit the earth." Meekness is the secret of possessing everything! And when you possess everything, you do not have to fret over what others have or what they are doing. King Saul's restlessness was caused by his envy of David, and he literally killed himself chasing David and trying to keep him from getting the crown. Saul's power was not under control, and it destroyed him.

"The meek shall inherit the earth." You inherit something because somebody dies and leaves a bequest to you in his will. In this case, it is *we* who die—die to self—that we might grow in meekness; and as we grow in meekness, we share the rich inheritance that we have in Christ. There is no need for us to assert ourselves to impress others, boast about ourselves, or even defend ourselves, because the Father has all that under His control. The meek person is never envious of others because of what they have. "A little that a righteous man hath is better than the riches of many wicked" (Psalm 37:16). "I have been young, and now am old; yet have I not seen the righteous forsaken, nor his seed begging bread" (Psalm 37:25).

The great enemy of meekness is impatience. This is why the psalmist admonishes us: "Wait on the Lord, and keep his way, and he shall exalt thee to inherit the land" (v. 34). Joseph waited on the Lord, and one day he was exalted and inherited the land. David waited on the Lord and endured the persecution of Saul, and one day God exalted him to inherit the land. The meek person does not fret or fight; he simply submits and waits, knowing that God's timing is perfect. "The trying of your faith worketh patience. But let patience have her perfect work, that ye may be perfect and entire, wanting nothing" (James 1:3-4). Wanting nothing? That means having everything!

"Blessed are the meek: for they shall inherit the earth."

Blessed are they which do hunger and thirst after righteousness, for they shall be filled.

(Matthew 5:6)

As the hart panteth after the water brooks, so panteth my soul after thee, O God. My soul thirsteth for God, for the living God: when shall I come and appear before God?

(Psalm 42:1-2)

O God, thou art my God; early will I seek thee: my soul thirsteth for thee, my flesh longeth for thee in a dry and thirsty land, where no water is.

(Psalm 63:1)

Every one that thirsteth, come ye to the waters, and he that hath no money; come ye, buy, and eat; yea, come, buy wine and milk without money and without price. Wherefore do ye spend money for that which is not bread? and your labour for that which satisfieth not? hearken diligently unto me, and eat ye that which is good, and let your soul delight itself in fatness.

(Isaiah 55:1-2)

6

The Hungry and Thirsty

Food and water are necessities, not luxuries. This was especially true in Palestine in Jesus' day. Both food and water were used carefully and never wasted. The owning of a well and the cultivating of a field were matters of life and death. So, when Jesus linked together hunger, thirst, and righteousness, He was telling the people that righteousness is not a luxury; it is a necessity. Our physical life depends upon food and water; our spiritual life depends upon righteousness.

HUNGER

Doctors tell us that we are what we eat. This principle is true not only of the body but also of the soul. The outer man depends upon food and water, and the inner man depends upon righteousness. The inner man of the spirit has appetites that must be satisfied, and if they are not satisfied with the spiritual food that God has provided, then they become sickly and weak. If the inner man is to function as he should, he must be fed.

The inner man has a sense of sight. Paul prayed for the Ephesians that the "eyes of [their] understanding [be] enlightened" (Ephesians 1:18). Our Lord lamented that although His disciples had eyes they saw not (Mark 8:18). His counsel to the church at Laodicea was that they anoint their eyes with eye salve that they might see (Revelation 3:18).

The inner man also has a spiritual sense of hearing. "Who hath ears to hear, let him hear!" Christ's sheep hear His voice and follow Him (John 10:3-4), but they will not follow the voice of a stranger (John 10:5). Immature Christians are "dull of hearing" because they do not exercise their spiritual senses (Hebrews 5:11-14).

There is also a spiritual sense of taste. "O taste and see that the Lord is good!" (Psalm 34:8). "If so be ye have tasted that the Lord is gracious" (1 Peter 2:3). The soul has its hunger and thirst; those desires were built into man at creation. "Thou hast set eternity in their heart" (Ecclesiastes 3:11, ASV*). Augustine said it perfectly: "Thou hast made us for Thyself, and our hearts are restless until they rest in Thee." Just as it is normal for the deer to thirst after water, so it is natural for man to thirst after God. He may not know that his thirst is for God, and he will probably try to satisfy that thirst with a substitute that will leave him with more thirst. But a thirst for God is what it is, just the same. God has put eternity in our hearts, and the temporal cannot satisfy.

The person who has trusted Christ has found the answer to that hidden hunger and thirst in his life; for Jesus Christ is the bread of life, and He alone can satisfy. "I am the bread of life: he that cometh to me shall never hunger; and he that believeth on me shall never thirst" (John 6:35). Jesus told the Samaritan woman at the well, "Whosoever drinketh of this water shall thirst again: but who-

American Standard Version.

soever drinketh of the water that I shall give him shall never thirst" (John 4:13-14).

The presence of hunger and thirst in the life is a good thing. To begin with, hunger and thirst are evidences of life. Dead people have no appetites. The unsaved person has an appetite for sin; he is compared to a dog licking his own vomit and a pig wallowing in the mire (2 Peter 2:22). The Christian is a sheep—a clean animal—that enjoys the green pastures and the still waters. The kind of appetite we have is an indication of the kind of heart we have. The heart of the unbeliever, although it was created with a hunger for God, tries to satisfy itself with "that which is not bread." Jeremiah says it mostly vividly: "They have forsaken me the fountain of living waters, and hewed them out cisterns, broken cisterns, that can hold no water" (2:13).

The believer who hungers and thirsts after righteousness is giving evidence not only of life but also of health. One of the first symptoms of sickness is loss of appetite, and one of the first signs of regained health after sickness is the return of appetite. When the infection of unconfessed sin is at work in the life of the disobedient Christian, he loses his appetite for spiritual things. He spends his money on that which is not bread, and he feeds on substitutes. But when the Christian confesses his sins and is restored to fellowship, his appetite for the things of God returns.

Were it not for hunger and thirst, we would be unable to live and work. Hunger is a sign that the body needs fuel. If we could continue to live and work without knowing that we needed food and water, we would kill ourselves. Just as pain is a sign that there is something wrong with the body, so hunger and thirst are signs that something is needed by the body. The spiritual meaning is not difficult to see: a hunger and thirst for the things of God is preparation for life and service.

It is tragic when people hunger and thirst for the wrong things. The prodigal son yearned for excitement and popularity, and he found them in the far country. But they did not last, and he soon found himself hungry again; but this time there was nothing to satisfy the hunger. "How many hired servants of my father's have bread enough and to spare" (Luke 15:17). He was so hungry that even bread would have satisfied him! Up till the time the famine hit him, he would have settled for nothing less than the finest luxuries the far country had to offer. First John 2:15-17 warns that our spiritual appetite can never be satisfied by the world—the desires of the flesh, the desires of the eyes, and the pride of life. All of those things are passing away, "but he that doeth the will of God abideth for ever." This reminds us of our Lord's statement to His disciples when they returned to Sychar after going for food: "My meat is to do the will of him that sent me, and to finish his work" (John 4:34). Jesus fed on the will of God; that is what satisfied Him.

What are the hungers in your life? What are the longings that you yearn to have satisfied? If the desires are out of the will of God, to satisfy them means disappointment and judgment. If they are in the will of God, to satisfy them means enjoyment, growth, and fulfillment.

HOLINESS

Jesus tells us that the way to be satisfied ("filled") is to hunger and thirst after *righteousness*. It is a hunger for holiness that fills the soul and satisfies the appetite of the inner man. It is too bad that we desire lesser things, including lesser blessings. The people of Israel "lusted exceedingly in the wilderness. . . . And he gave them their request; but sent leanness into their soul" (Psalm 106:14-15). Had Israel listened to God's Word and cultivated an appetite for His will, God would have "fed them also with the finest of the wheat: and with honey out of the rock" (Psalm 81:16).

Theologians tell us that there are three kinds of holiness: imputed, which is justification; imparted, which is sanctification; and eternal, which is glorification. When the sinner trusts Christ, he is declared righteous; this is imputed holiness. As a result of this decision, his life changes, and he shares imparted holiness. The righteousness of Christ becomes a part of his daily life. The person who professes salvation but practices sin is not born of God (1 John 4:1-10). The Christian is not only justified by faith (Romans 5:1), but he is justified unto life (Romans 5:18). Justification is much more than a legal matter recorded on the books of heaven. It is a personal matter that involves a living relationship with God and results in a living revelation of God in our everyday lives.

But what is holiness? To the Pharisees, holiness was conformity to rules; it was an external thing that completely overlooked the needs of the inner man. That explains why Jesus warned, "Except your righteousness shall exceed the righteousness of the scribes and Pharisees, ye shall in no case enter into the kingdom of heaven" (Matthew 5:20). A mere external piety, born of pride and nurtured by the praise of men, is not holiness. If the Beatitudes teach us anything, it is that holiness begins in the heart.

The words *holy* and *whole* belong to the same family. To be holy involves wholeness. Sin divides and destroys, but holiness unites and builds. Holiness is the basic attribute of God: "God is light, and in him is no darkness at all" (1 John 1:5). When you hunger for holiness, you hunger for God. "My soul thirsteth for thee!" And to have God in your life means wholeness; He puts everything together. "Through Him all things are held together" (Colossians 1:17, Williams). When the prodigal son hungered for material possessions and thrills, everything fell apart.

When he came to himself and returned to his father, everything was made whole again. In fact, what he was looking for in the far country *he found right at home.*

To be righteous means to be right—right with God, right with self, and right with others. When you hunger and thirst for God, then you are causing the inner man to function as God made him to function. Your spiritual senses are exercised and developed (Hebrews 5:14). "Exercise thyself rather unto godliness" (1 Timothy 4:7). There is a unity to the life of the person whose deepest desire is to know and please God and to enjoy Him. Instead of running from one substitute to another, seeking inner satisfaction, he says, "All my springs are in thee" (Psalm 87:7). "Lord, to whom shall we go? thou hast the words of eternal life" (John 6:68).

As the inner man is satisfied with holiness, he becomes increasingly dissatisfied with sin. "Ye that love the Lord, hate evil" (Psalm 97:10). To begin with, the mind grows in its recognition of sin. The closer we get to the light, the easier it is to see the defilement. The more we are satisfied with God, the more we are dissatisfied with substitutes, including religious substitutes. The mind recognizes sin, and the heart is repulsed by sin. The dog returns to his vomit, and the sow wallows in the mire; but the sheep has nothing to do with either one. The mind recognizes sin, the heart is repulsed by sin, and the will refuses sin. It is the appreciation of the excellent that motivates the believer to refuse the cheap and the defiled.

When you control hunger, you control life. Find out what a man's deep appetites are, provide the satisfaction, and you control his life. Dictators and propagandists have followed this principle for centuries. If the appetite is not there, create one. The advertising agencies sell their services for this very purpose. It is unfortunate when our churches create appetites for lesser things—for religious entertainment instead of spiritual food, for multiplied activities instead of spiritual ministries, for sentimental music instead of the spiritual songs of Zion. Having once created the appetite, they must satisfy it; and this plunges our churches into that terrible maelstrom of promotion, celebrities, statistics, and instant results. The sheep need to be led by the quiet waters, but they find themselves drowning in the whirlpool called success.

If a man wants to master a skill, he must have a deep desire to do so, or he will fail. Perhaps his motives are mixed, but if there is a hunger for achievement, he will have an easier time. Change the hunger, and you change the man; control the hunger, and you control the man. Jesus Christ wants to create in us a deep hunger for God, a hunger for holiness. It is this hunger that will change and control our lives as we satisfy it in Jesus Christ.

HAPPINESS

It must have come as a surprise to His listeners when Jesus equated holiness and happiness. He promised that they would be *blessed* if they hungered and thirsted after righteousness. They had seen the Pharisees practice their brand of holiness, and the Pharisees did not seem too happy. There seemed to be no touch of blessing in their lives. The people in that day, like people today, equated holy living with misery! Why did they do that?

For one thing, they had the wrong idea of holiness. They thought of it in terms of negatives, for that was all that they saw in the Pharisees. The Pharisees were better known for what they were *against* rather than what they were *for*. Unfortunately, some Christians are that way today. Their Christian experience is a painful bondage instead of a glorious liberty. Jesus enjoyed life, even though life for Him was difficult. He was happy because He was holy. The Pharisees were neither happy nor holy, and Jesus pointed that out to them; so they crucified Him. His joyful, holy life so exposed their brittle piety that He became their enemy. Because the Pharisees had a faulty view of holiness, they robbed themselves of happiness.

But they also had a faulty view of sin, and a person with a faulty view of sin will not know how to find the righteousness that satisfies the inner man. Righteousness for them was a matter of meeting certain external regulations; and sin was simply not obeying those regulations. They never looked deep within their hearts as Paul did when he said, "O wretched man that I am! who shall deliver me from the body of this death?" (Romans 7:24). A wrong view of sin and a wrong view of holiness go together. When Isaiah saw the holiness of God, he immediately saw his own sinfulness, and he cried out, "Woe is me! for I am undone!" (Isaiah 6:5). The apostle John once rested upon Jesus' bosom, but when the aged apostle saw the vision of the risen Priest-King, he fell at His feet as though he were dead (Revelation 1:17). The unbeliever cannot understand how the Christian can behold the holiness of God, then confess his own helplessness, and out of this experience find happiness. But, understand it or not, this is the divine formula: holiness, helplessness, happiness.

We must grow in our love for holiness. No doubt at the beginning of our spiritual walk we seek righteousness in order to avoid pain, the way a little child obeys so that he might not receive a spanking. This is a negative approach to building character, but it is the best way for a child. We have to begin somewhere. As we grow in grace, we discover that holy living not only avoids chastening, but it also brings positive reward. "No good thing will he withhold from them that walk uprightly" (Psalm 84:11). The danger here, of course, is that we are more concerned with the blessing than the Blesser, and holy living must be the result of a *personal* relationship. When we discover this truth, we graduate into the third level: we seek holiness in order to please the Father. The result of this experience is to reach an even higher level: we seek a holy life because we love God and want to glorify Him. The Pharisees loved themselves and sought to glorify themselves, and, as Jesus said, they had their reward.

Seeking to please the Father and cultivating a hunger for holiness brings about a remarkable change in our lives: we become more like Him. After all, we are what we eat; and if our food is to do the will of God, then our lives become the will of God. The will of God is not simply something we do; it is something we are. Holiness becomes to us the beauty of God, and we want that beauty for our own lives. You would never have looked at the Pharisees and yearned to have what they had; but if you had watched Jesus come and go among the people, you would have hungered for what He was. The publicans and sinners were attracted by the holiness of Christ; they were repelled by the religious piety of the Pharisees (Luke 15:1-2).

One of the essential differences between mere outward piety and true holiness is that piety makes you conform to a system, whereas true holiness conforms you to Christ *and develops your own individuality.* The Pharisees were each like the other; the disciples were individual and distinctive. The more we become like Christ, the more we are liberated to become our best selves. Abraham and Moses were both men of God; yet each was different from the other. Spurgeon and Moody were both men of God, deeply taught in the lessons of God's grace; yet neither was like the other one. The "beauty of holiness" (Psalm 29:2) is not by imitation but by impartation and incarnation. "Christ liveth in me" (Galatians 2:20).

HARMONY

How does holiness bring happiness?

If knowing God, enjoying God, and becoming like God is our highest desire, then the fulfilling of that desire will bring us the highest happiness. "They shall be filled" is Christ's promise; and that word *filled* carries with it a double meaning: "satisfied" and "controlled by." If we hunger and thirst after God's righteousness, then He will satisfy that hunger; and when He has satisfied it, we will discover that our lives are controlled by His righteousness in all that we do. Seeking to become like Him pleases both us and the Father. The higher we climb by His grace on this highway of holiness, the less satisfied we are with the things that make others happy. The disciples had come a long way in their spiritual walk when they could pray, "Lord, show us the Father, and it is enough for us" (John 14:8, NASB).

Holiness brings happiness not only by sparing us the pain of sin and its consequences, but by purifying our hearts and minds and giving us an appetite for the eternal. "As for me, I will behold thy face in righteousness: I shall be satisfied, when I awake, with thy likeness" (Psalm 17:15). As we become more like Christ, we share more of His joy.

Too many Christians believe they can satisfy their hunger for holiness by multiplied activities and special endeavors, when each of these could do more harm than good. It is usually not in the multiplying of activities but in the *simplifying of life* that we experience the deepest satisfaction in Christ. This does not mean that we necessarily do less; rather, it means that what we do is centered in Christ so that He has the preeminence. "This one thing I do" (Philippians 3:13). "Martha, Martha, thou art careful and troubled about many things: but one thing is needful" (Luke 10:41-42). "One thing have I desired of the Lord, that will I seek after; that I may dwell in the house of the Lord all the days of my life, to behold the beauty of the Lord, and to enquire in his temple" (Psalm 27:4).

Growing in holiness simplifies our lives, unifies our lives, and satisfies our lives. No more of the broken cisterns: we are drinking at the pure river of the water of life! No more of the flesh-pots of Egypt: we have the bread of life! The praises of men fall on deaf ears: we want only the approval of God. The wealth of this world means little to us, for we rejoice in the riches of grace in Christ Jesus.

Growing in holiness, however, does not mean that we lose the good things of this world; rather, it means that we receive them back *and enjoy them more.* It is God "who giveth us richly all things to enjoy" (1 Timothy 6:17). Abraham placed Isaac on the altar and, in the will of God, died to self; but Abraham received him back to enjoy him in a deeper way than ever before. Jesus enjoyed playing with the children, feasting at the table, watching the birds and the lilies, and doing the everyday tasks of life. True holiness (which is wholeness) touches all of life, not merely a part. The Pharisees fasted twice a week and accused Jesus of being a glutton and a drunk. But their fasting was not an exercise in holiness; consequently, their fasting was sin. Our Lord's feasting was in the holy will of God because all of His life was controlled by that will. Holiness always involves *wholeness*—the whole person, the whole of life. "Whether therefore ye eat or drink, or whatsoever ye do, do all to the glory of God" (1 Corinthians 10:31). The Pharisee could never be happy, because he was not whole and his life was not whole. He was trying to patch his old garment with new cloth, and the seams would not hold. Jesus wore the seamless garment of holiness—wholeness—and walked in the joy of the Lord.

There is no holy living apart from the holy Son of God, the holy Word of God, and the Holy Spirit of God; they go together. The Spirit of God reveals the Son of God through the Word of God. If you have a hunger for holiness, then you will read the Word of God, meditate on it, and make it a vital part of your life. In the Word of God you will see the Son of God; and when you do, the Spirit of God will transform you so that you become more and more like Him. "But we all, with unveiled face beholding as in a mirror the glory of the Lord, are being transformed into the same image from glory to glory, just as from the Lord, the Spirit" (2 Corinthians 3:18, NASB). Moses did not get a shining face by looking at himself: he spent forty days gazing at the glory of the Lord. Stephen looked away from the hateful faces of men and gazed upon the face of Christ, and his own face radiated the glory of God.

There is no escaping the fact that the men and women of God in the Bible and church history dared to reject the comfortable piety of their age and abandoned themselves to experience the holiness of God. They hungered and thirsted after righteousness, and God satisfied them. They paid a price, but the reward was worth it. No more could they return to the broken cisterns—even the religious cisterns—once they had drunk deeply of the living waters. The heroes of faith in Hebrews 11 were not persecuted because of their religion, but because what they believed so affected the way they behaved that they became a threat to the religious conformists around them. After the Exodus Israel was constantly wanting to go back to Egypt. They forgot the slavery; they only remembered the leeks, the onions, and the garlic! But while they were looking back, Moses was looking ahead; and he "endured, as seeing him who is invisible" (Hebrews 11:27). Moses had a different appetite from that of the people, and therefore he had a different ambition. No wonder holy men and women of God have always been persecuted by the religious crowd and utterly rejected by the people of the world! They had "trial of cruel mockings and scourgings, yea, moreover of bonds and imprisonment: they were stoned, they were sawn asunder, were tempted, were slain with the sword: they wandered about in sheepskins and goatskins; being destitute, afflicted, tormented; (of whom the world was not worthy)" (Hebrews

11:36-38). And all because they hungered and thirsted after righteousness.

If we are to reign in life and live like kings, we must have God's righteousness, imputed and imparted. God's grace reigns in our lives *through righteousness* (Romans 5:21). Jesus Christ, our High Priest, belongs to the order of Melchizedek—"king of righteousness." The prodigal son became a slave when he rebelled against his father and lived to please himself. When he returned to his father and submitted to righteousness, he experienced grace and began to live like a king.

All of God's blessings are the by-products of His righteousness. "But seek ye first the kingdom of God, and his righteousness; and all these things shall be added unto you" (Matthew 6:33). "All these things"—such as food, clothing, shelter, income, husband, wife. When we live for God's rule and God's righteousness in our lives, then we enjoy everything else!

There is no shortcut to happiness or holiness. We must begin with hunger—a hunger for holiness, a deep desire to be more like Christ. God promises to satisfy this hunger, and it is our responsibility to seek to develop this appetite for the righteousness of God. We are what we eat. "Blessed are they which do hunger and thirst after righteousness: for they shall be filled."

Blessed are the merciful: for they shall obtain mercy.
(Matthew 5:7)

But the wisdom that is from above is first pure, then peaceable, gentle, and easy to be intreated, full of mercy and good fruits.
(James 3:17)

He that sheweth mercy, with cheerfulness.
(Romans 12:8)

Put on therefore, as the elect of God, holy and beloved, bowels of mercies.
(Colossians 3:12)

Which now of these three, thinkest thou, was neighbour unto him that fell among the thieves? And he said, He that shewed mercy on him.
(Luke 10:36-37)

7

The Merciful

The Roman world did not admire mercy. They admired justice, courage, self-control, and wisdom, but not mercy. The philosophers called mercy "a disease of the soul," something to be abhorred and ashamed of if you expected to be a success. Slaves were treated like pieces of used furniture, and the position of women and children was far from ideal. If a woman gave birth to a daughter or a sickly son, the father had the privilege of rejecting the child and having it exposed to die. A temperamental master could, in a fit of anger, maim or even kill a slave. An enemy was an enemy, and the best enemy was a dead enemy.

Jesus Christ and the gospel began to change all of that. Jesus taught and practiced mercy, and He commanded His followers to show mercy. But when mercy was practiced by Jesus and His followers, it was a revelation of power, not weakness. Instead of being a sickness of the soul, mercy became the very health of their Christian experience.

Our world today is not too far removed spiritually from the Roman world in which Jesus gave the Beatitudes. People are still treated like things, power is the supreme deity, and success is the most important thing in life. How can a person practice mercy in a competitive society? Yet this is exactly what Jesus commands us to do!

GOD'S MERCY

According to the theologians, God has two kinds of attributes: absolute and relative. The absolute attributes describe what God is like in Himself, totally apart from His creation. God is love even if there are no human beings around to know about it. God is truth, and God is holy. These are essential characteristics of His being. But when man came on the scene, God had to relate these attributes to him; and hence, we have what the theologians call the "relative attributes." Truth becomes faithfulness, holiness becomes justice, and love becomes grace and mercy. Mercy is one of the spiritual bridges God has built so that He can relate to you and me; and mercy is a bridge you and I must build if we are going to relate lovingly to others.

God's mercy and grace grow out of His love. Nobody is saved because God loves him, for God loves the whole world. Sinners are saved because of God's grace and mercy, His love in action. It is easy to remember the difference between grace and mercy. God in His grace gives me what I do not deserve, and in His mercy He does not give me what I do deserve! In one sense, grace is positive, whereas mercy is negative, although this should not be carried too far. "It is of the Lord's mercies that we are not consumed" (Lamentations 3:22). "The Lord being merciful unto [Lot]" (Genesis 19:16). "Lord, have mercy on my son!" (Matthew 17:15). It is mercy that pities and grace that pardons.

There are several factors involved in this experience of mercy. It begins with pain: somebody hurts us unjustly, and we must respond to this hurt. If we have no power, then all we can do is give in; but if we have the power to retaliate, then we must decide what to do. You cannot show mercy unless you have the power to hurt. Suppose the person deserves to be hurt? Suppose his offense against us is so serious that we feel we must teach him a lesson? We have the power to hurt him back: should we use it? At this point, love enters the picture, not to cancel truth, but to control it. We are hurt; we have the power and (we believe) the right to hurt the one who hurt us. But because of God's love, we show mercy: we do not give the offender what he deserves. This demands faith; we must leave the offender and his offense in the hands of God. "Dearly beloved, avenge not yourselves" (Romans 12:19). What is the result of this painful experience? Growth! We share in the "fellowship of his sufferings" (Philippians 3:10) and become more like Him.

These, then, are the links in the chain of mercy: pain, power, truth, love, faith, growth. We suffer because of another's sin, but we choose to use our power for growth instead of retaliation. It is the act of faith that shows mercy that converts pain into spiritual growth. It is love that makes us want to exercise this faith; and it is the Holy Spirit within who gives us this love.

It is an awesome thought that when I show mercy, I am practicing one of the attributes of God. Mercy puts me into the place of God in somebody's life! The Beatitudes begin with the right attitude toward myself—poor in spirit. The next step is a right attitude toward my sin—I mourn. Then, a right attitude toward God's Word—"Blessed are the meek." This creates within me a deep desire for God's righteousness, and He gives it to me when I trust Christ. The first three Beatitudes are preparation for the miracle of the fourth when we, by faith, receive the very righteousness of God. And, having received His righteousness, we then begin *to be like God*: "Blessed are the merciful." "Be ye therefore followers [imitators] of God, as dear children" (Ephesians 5:1). Having received His divine nature, we begin to manifest His divine attributes; and mercy is one of His attributes.

MAN'S MERCY

Perhaps the best way to understand mercy is to see it in action.

Our first example is in Genesis 14, the story of Abraham's courageous rescue of his nephew Lot. To begin with, Lot had no business in Sodom. If he had been a spiritually minded man, he would have walked with Abraham and obeyed the Lord. But he decided to move into Sodom. When Sodom was attacked by the enemy kings, Lot had to suffer the consequences. He and his family were taken captive, and all their possessions were confiscated. When the word got to Abraham, the patriarch immediately gathered his servants and, with the help of God, went to battle and rescued Lot. That was an act of mercy. Abraham could have said, "Well, the young man is stubborn and didn't know when he was well-off. Let him stew in his own juice!" Had not Abraham given Lot first choice of the land? Had not Lot's choice been a foolish one? Then why rescue him? Because it was the merciful thing to do to a brother (Genesis 14:16). Abraham had the power to hurt Lot, and certainly Lot had hurt Abraham; yet, in faith and love, Abraham chose to show mercy. In the New Testament, Abraham is honored as the great man of faith, and rightly so; but faith plus love equals mercy, and Abraham had all three.

A second example is Joseph. If your brothers treated you the way Joseph's brothers treated him, what would you do to them once they were under your power? They had lied about him, caused him to suffer, and sold him as a slave! Most of them even wanted to kill him! But now the tables were turned: the brothers were bowing before the prime minister of Egypt—Joseph—and he had the power to hurt them. What a temptation! Joseph faced two great temptations in his life, and in both instances he came out victorious. He was tempted to a sin of the flesh by Potiphar's wife, but he fled from her and kept himself pure. He was tempted to a sin of the spirit by his brothers—he could have taken vengeance upon them—but instead, he went off and wept and then came back and showed mercy. To be sure, Joseph so dealt with his brothers that he was sure their hearts were changed before he openly forgave them; but even this was an evidence of his mercy. Joseph was neither a prodigal son nor an elder brother; he did not yield to either a sin of the flesh or a sin of the spirit. Instead, he was like Jesus Christ, the Son of God, who prayed, "Father, forgive them, for they know not what they do" (Luke 23:34).

Our third example of true mercy is David, the man after God's own heart—and therefore the man who revealed God's own heart. David was the true, anointed king of Israel, even though Saul was still exercising power and using that power to persecute David and his men. On two occasions, David had Saul in his power and could have killed him (1 Samuel 24, 26), but he refused to do so. Instead, he showed mercy. Some of his men wanted David to kill their enemy; they argued that God had brought Saul into their power. But David knew that his real power was not in killing but in showing mercy. Saul had reigned in malice and hatred, but David would reign in love and mercy. In fact, when Saul finally was killed, David sang a lamentation and made no mention whatsoever of Saul's hatred toward him (2 Samuel 1:17-27). "The beauty of Is-

rael is slain upon thy high places: how are the mighty fall-
en!" (v. 19).

In each of these instances, there were both pain and
the power to retaliate. But there was also "faith which
worketh by love" (Galatians 5:6), and this resulted in
mercy. The act of mercy put the one showing mercy on
the throne—for it was Abraham who was in control, not
Lot; and it was Joseph and David who reigned in life, not
their persecutors. We might add that Joseph's experience
of mercy made life happier and easier for his brothers,
and they reigned in life with him. When you show mercy,
it not only helps you to grow and reign, but it also helps
others. If, like Saul, they refuse the mercy, then God will
judge them. If, like Joseph's brothers, they accept the
mercy, God will bless them. The choice is theirs, not ours.

Mercy and the Cross

The greatest example of showing mercy is seen, of
course, in the life of the Lord Jesus Christ. How simple it
would have been for Him to answer His enemies with
deeds of judgmental power instead of words of grace. The
intensity of their opposition increased the closer He came
to Calvary, and yet the strength of His mercy matched the
intensity of their hatred. Not that He refused to expose
their sins: the sermon in Matthew 23 is proof enough that
mercy does not sweep the dust under the rug. When the
chief priests and rulers had Him arrested, they gave Him
in that act a glorious opportunity to avenge Himself. Had
He done so, nobody would have criticized Him. Instead,
He willingly submitted to the mob and rebuked His impetuous disciple. "Thinkest thou that I cannot now pray to
my Father, and he shall presently give me more then
twelve legions of angels?" (Matthew 26:53).

We see in Jesus Christ the fulfillment of Psalm 85:10:
"Mercy and truth are met together; righteousness and

peace have kissed each other." He knew the truth about sinners and even exposed the truth about sinners, and yet He showed mercy to them! The feeble mercy that cultured men show to each other is usually based on ignorance or deception. "If we knew all we would forgive all," is their motto. Or, "I am just as sinful as you are, so I will show mercy to you because you will show mercy to me." Although it is better than nothing, the humanistic approach to mercy falls far short of the divine ideal.

Jesus showed mercy, yet He certainly could not plead either ignorance or sin. Jesus "needed not that any should testify of man: for he knew what was in man" (John 2:25). "Which of you convinceth me of sin?" (John 8:46). He was able to show mercy *because of His work on the cross.* It was there that mercy and truth met together and righteousness and peace kissed each other. His death at Calvary was a testimony to the truth that we are sinners, and yet it was also a triumph over sin in that it opened up the fountains of the mercy of God. There is a "judgment without mercy" (James 2:13), but it as not at Calvary. On the cross, there was judgment *with* mercy.

This fact suggests that you and I, if we are not discerning, can practice a kind of counterfeit mercy that denies truth and righteousness and that does not lead to peace. Perhaps this is the kind of mercy that David showed Absalom when he let him off easy and thus sowed the seeds of rebellion in the boy's heart. David's mourning over Absalom's death is one of the most poignant scenes in all literature, but nothing could have changed Absalom's character, let alone his tragic destiny. Whenever mercy is extended, it must be on the basis of truth; and David's mercy toward his son was not on that basis. There is no record that Absalom ever repented (where truth comes in) or that David ever encouraged him to repent (where righteousness comes in). The whole transaction was shallow and sentimental, not spiritual.

We have too many transactions of the same tragic character in our churches today.

Another example of counterfeit mercy is Ahab's
treatment of Ben-Hadad (1 Kings 20:32). Ordered to slay
the enemy king, Ahab spared him in what seemed to be a
great act of mercy. But mercy and truth did not meet that
day, and the result was not righteousness or peace. The
result was sin and war. Ahab spared his enemy in order
to feed his own ego and become a great hero. He gave no
thought to the will of God or the glory of God.

To extend mercy means to withhold judgment. Mercy
means that God does not give us what we deserve. But
there can be no true mercy apart from justice; somebody
simply has to pay the price for sin. This is where the cross
comes in: "Who his own self bare our sins in his own
body on the tree" (1 Peter 2:24). God forgives us and
shows us mercy on the basis of His Son's sacrifice, and we
show mercy to others on that same basis. Were it not for
Calvary, mercy and truth could never meet together, and
righteousness and peace would never result.

"Father, forgive them, for they know not what they
do" (Luke 23:34). Of what were they ignorant? Of the
Person against whom they were sinning, for one thing.
"Now, brethren, I [know] that through ignorance ye did it,
as did also your rulers" (Acts 3:17). They were also ignorant of the enormity of their sin. They were rejecting God
and making God suffer! Ignorance does not remove guilt,
but it does mitigate the sentence. Our Lord's prayer for
the nation did not automatically result in the personal forgiveness of every man who had been involved in His arrest and crucifixion. But it did postpone God's judgment
and give the nation another opportunity to repent. That is
mercy.

It is the cross that makes mercy available to us and
through us. We must never extend mercy on the basis of
our own "spirituality" but rather on the basis of His fin-

ished sacrifice. If the mercy we show bypasses the cross, then it also bypasses truth and righteousness, and it can never lead to peace. "But the wisdom that is from above is first pure, then peaceable" (James 3:17). "Peace at any price" is never a basis for mercy. "Having made peace through the blood of his cross" (Colossians 1:20) is the only true basis for mercy. How can we tell the one from the other in actual practice? Counterfeit mercy always inflates the ego of the believer, but true mercy humbles him and gives God the glory.

EXPERIENCING MERCY

You cannot extend mercy until you have received it. Mercy is not a quality natural to man; it must be received as a gift from God. "Not by works of righteousness which we have done, but according to his mercy he saved us" (Titus 3:5). But the receiving of mercy cannot be a mere commercial transaction between me and God; *I must experience it in my heart.* The problem with the unmerciful servant in Christ's parable (Matthew 18:21-35) was that he looked upon the king's mercy as something that could have been earned if only there had been time enough to work. "Lord, have patience with me, and I will pay thee all!" The man was never really broken by the debt of his sins, and therefore his attitude was that of a prankster who had been let off the hook and not of a rebel who had been delivered from death. He received mercy in a commercial manner; he did not experience mercy in a spiritual manner. For this reason he was unable to extend mercy to his fellow worker, who owed him a paltry sum when compared with his own debt.

The need to experience mercy may help to explain the Lord's Supper. Most of us want to forget the death of a loved one, yet Jesus wants us to remember His death. Why? In coming to the Lord's Supper, we must first examine ourselves (1 Corinthians 11:28), and that means to be confronted with mercy and truth. We must confess the truth about ourselves, and then claim His mercy in forgiveness. We do not come to the Lord's Table to remember our sins; we come to remember Christ. But we cannot eat and drink in a worthy manner if we do not tell the truth to ourselves and to God. The broken bread and the cup remind us of the mercy of God. "Thou shalt remember that thou wast a bondman in the land of Egypt, and the Lord thy God redeemed thee" (Deuteronomy 15:15). The Christian never says with the worldly sentimentalist, "I am a sinner, therefore, I can show mercy to you." Rather, he says, "I am a *forgiven* sinner, and because I have experienced mercy and truth at Calvary, I can extend mercy to you." Sins committed can never be the fountain for mercy. It is when sins are *forgiven* that "mercy and truth are met together."

But salvation is only the beginning; there must also be submission. Have you ever noticed that Romans 12 begins with surrender and ends with "Dearly beloved, avenge not yourselves?" Being a "living sacrifice" means *living the sacrifice of Christ.* It was while they were crucifying Him that He prayed, "Father, forgive them, for they know not what they do." Romans 12 does not stop with verse 2! It goes on to say, "Bless them which persecute you: bless, and curse not. . . . Recompense to no man evil for evil. . . . Dearly beloved, avenge not yourselves . . . . Be not overcome of evil, but overcome evil with good" (Romans 12:14, 17, 19, 21). David knew that it was not his privilege to exercise vengeance, so he left Saul in the hands of God. David showed mercy. Because he was submissive to the will of God, he was able to "give place unto" the wrath of God (Romans 12:19).

Besides salvation and submission, there is a third essential that we must possess if we are going to extend mercy, and that is suffering. When mercy and truth meet together, the result has to be suffering. The one extending mercy suffers because he experiences the hurt caused by his enemy; and the one receiving mercy suffers as he realizes what he has done and repents of his sin. Whenever you are dealing with sin, there is going to be pain. But the experience of mercy heals the wounds and turns the suffering into joy.

This principle is illustrated in John 8, where the Pharisees burst into our Lord's morning message and confront Him with the woman taken in the very act of adultery. The record indicates that there are several ways to deal with sin. There is the way of Moses, the way of law. "Now Moses in the law commanded us, that such should be stoned" (John 8:5). Law can never cleanse; it can only condemn. It cannot give power to keep from sinning; it can only inflict judgment after sin has been committed. Jesus rejected that way.

A second way to deal with sin is man's way: find the sinner, expose the sinner, and even use the sinner to accomplish your own selfish purposes—in other words, play God! Jesus dealt with this egotistical approach in one simple sentence: "He that is without sin among you, let him first cast a stone at her" (John 8:7).

If Moses' way is rejected, and if man's way is not accepted, then what is left? The Master's way. "Neither do I condemn thee: go, and sin no more" (John 8:11). Notice that Jesus did not deny the fact of sin. He knew she was a sinner, and she knew that she was a sinner. But mercy and truth met together that morning, and the result was a forgiven sinner. But think of what that cost Jesus! Think of how His holy soul was pained by her sin and by the self-righteous judgment of the religious leaders. And think of the suffering He would endure on the cross to make her cleansing possible! There can be no mercy without suffering, no pardon without pain.

The vindictive, defensive Christian is protecting himself; the merciful Christian is making himself vulnerable. The priest and Levite hurried past the half-dead traveler and saved themselves suffering and danger. (After all, those same robbers might still be around!) But the Good Samaritan made himself vulnerable; he deliberately exposed himself to suffering so that he might show mercy to the helpless victim. Expect to suffer as you share God's mercy, for even the Lord could not show mercy and escape suffering. But the suffering we experience is not destructive; it is the "fellowship of his sufferings" (Philippians 3:10). Some of David's greatest psalms came out of his painful experiences with Saul and Absalom. Some of your greatest songs will be born the same way.

<h2 style="text-align:center">EXTENDING MERCY TO OTHERS</h2>

"Blessed are the merciful: for they shall obtain mercy." What does it mean to obtain mercy? Certainly it does not mean that we *earn* mercy because we *extend* mercy, for such an idea is foreign to the Word of God. By its very definition, mercy cannot be earned any more than grace can be earned. The Beatitude is saying: "When you experience and share mercy, then your heart is in such a condition that you can receive more mercy to share with others." In other words, Jesus is not asking us to be merciful occasionally; He is asking us to be constant channels of mercy. "Give, and it shall be given unto you" (Luke 6:38). By extending mercy, we open our hearts to receive mercy; and having received, we can share again and again.

The Christian is surrounded by mercy. He can say, "Surely goodness and mercy shall follow me all the days of my life" (Psalm 23:6). When he looks ahead, he remembers the words of Jude 21—"looking for the mercy of our Lord Jesus Christ unto eternal life." As he begins each new day, he can say: "It is of the Lord's mercies that we are not consumed, because his compassions fail not. They are new every morning: great is thy faithfulness" (Lamentations 3:22-23).

It is a basic fact of theology that God responds to us on the basis of the condition of the heart. "With the merciful thou wilt shew thyself merciful; with an upright man thou wilt shew thyself upright; with the pure thou wilt shew thyself pure; and with the froward thou wilt shew thyself froward" (Psalm 18:25-26). Jacob was a schemer and a fighter, so God had to wrestle with him and break him before He could bless him. Peter was an impetuous, self-sufficient man, so Jesus had to let him plunge into denial and defeat before He could make him a success. When once we begin to cultivate one of the spiritual graces, *God always provides more*. When we show mercy, He gives mercy; and thus we have more mercy to show.

When a Christian shows mercy, he experiences liberation. He is set free from grudges that drain the strength and unsettle the mind. The unmerciful servant in the parable (Matthew 18:21-35) put himself and his family into prison because he could not forgive a friend. The most miserable prison in the world is the prison we make for ourselves when we refuse to show mercy. Our thoughts become shackled, our emotions are chained, the will is almost paralyzed. But when we show mercy, all of those bonds are broken, and we enter into a joyful liberty that frees us to share God's love with others. This blessing of freedom is one way that we receive mercy as we show mercy. It is a blessed by-product of obeying God.

You can be sure that there will always be opportunities to show mercy. We never grow out of this privilege. But what a glorious experience it is! How thrilling it is to go through life sharing God's mercy and not having to judge people to see if they are "worthy" of what we have to offer. We stop looking at the externals and begin to see people through the merciful eyes of Christ. Every Christian we meet is a person in whom Jesus lives; every lost soul we meet is a person for whom Jesus died. In both cases, we have candidates for God's mercy.

The only way God could get His mercy to this world was through His Son. The Son of God had to become flesh before mercy and truth could meet together. It is the same today: mercy in the abstract means nothing—*it must always be incarnate in human flesh*. The evasive lawyer wanted Jesus to discuss the abstract doctrine of "Who is my neighbor?" But Jesus forced him to see one half-dead stranger at the side of the road, and one hated alien who showed mercy to that stranger. The world cannot see mercy apart from the people who experience it and share it.

You and I are to be those people.

Blessed are the pure in heart: for they shall see God.

(Matthew 5:8)

The light of the body is the eye: if therefore thine eye be single, thy whole body shall be full of light. But if thine eye be evil, thy whole body shall be full of darkness.

(Matthew 6:22-23)

I beseech thee, shew me thy glory.

(Exodus 33:18)

No man hath seen God at any time; the only begotten Son, which is in the bosom of the Father, he hath declared him.

(John 1:18)

O God, thou art my God; early will I seek thee . . . to see thy power and thy glory, so as I have seen thee in the sanctuary.

(Psalm 63:1-2)

They shall see his face.

(Revelation 22:4)

8

The Pure in Heart

At some point in life, each of us must decide what is his highest joy; for the thing that delights us directs us. Generally speaking, a child finds his delight in what he has; a youth in what he does; and an adult in what he is. The first lives for possessions, the second for experiences, and the third for character. We do not condemn the child and the youth for living as they do, because neither has reached maturity; but we would certainly wonder at an adult who lived on those lower levels. The adult should know that possessions and experiences are empty apart from character. What we *are* determines how much we enjoy what we *have* and what we *do*.

Every person has an outlook on life; he is seeking his highest joy. Outlook determines outcome. Abraham lifted up his eyes and saw the stars and became the friend of God by faith. Lot lifted up his eyes and saw Sodom and became the friend of the world. Abraham inherited the city prepared for him by God, the city he had been seeking (Hebrews 11:13-16); but Lot lost everything when Sodom went up in smoke.

If life is to be rich and meaningful, then our joys must be the highest possible; and Jesus tells us that the highest joy possible is to see God.

What Is the "Heart"?

Let's begin with the word *heart*—"Blessed are the pure in heart: for they shall see God." Biblical psychology is not always as scientifically precise as we would like it to be. Paul writes about our "whole spirit and soul and body" (1 Thessalonians 5:23), and the theologians suggest that the spirit is God-consciousness, the soul is self-consciousness, and the body is world-consciousness. Some students further suggest that the soul includes the God-given functions of intellect, emotion, and will. These are convenient categories, but they may not always be consistent. Jesus tells us that the greatest commandment is to love God with all our heart, soul, mind, and strength, indicating *four* functions of personality.

Sometimes the Bible uses the word *heart* to indicate the emotions. "Let not your heart be troubled" (John 14:1). "This is nothing else but sorrow of heart" (Nehemiah 2:2). But the heart can also refer to the intellect. "Why reason ye these things in your hearts?" (Mark 2:8). Hebrews 4:12 states that the Word of God is a "discerner of the thoughts and intents of the heart." The heart also indicates the volitional function, the will. "But Daniel purposed in his heart that he would not defile himself" (Daniel 1:8). Jesus admonished His disciples, "Settle it therefore in your hearts, not to meditate before what ye shall answer" (Luke 21:14).

Putting it all together, you get the impression that *the heart* simply means *the inner man with his many functions.* This is the "master control" area of life. "Keep thy heart with all diligence, for out of it are the issues of life" (Proverbs 4:23). It is here that salvation is experienced:

"That if thou shalt confess with thy mouth the Lord Jesus [Jesus as Lord], and shalt believe in thine heart that God hath raised him from the dead, thou shalt be saved" (Romans 10:9). The Pharisees tried to please God, but they ignored the heart and majored on outward actions. "This people draweth nigh unto me with their mouth," said Jesus, "and honoureth me with their lips; but their heart is far from me" (Matthew 15:8).

The heart, of course, is the source of all our trouble. We are prone to blame people and circumstances, and even God, for the wrong things that we do; but the heart is really the culprit. "The heart is deceitful above all things, and desperately wicked: who can know it?" (Jeremiah 17:9). Neither time nor experience has changed the human heart. God's indictment before the Flood is just as valid today: "God saw that the wickedness of man was great in the earth, and that every imagination of the thoughts of his heart was only evil continually" (Genesis 6:5). Jesus spells it out in greater detail: "For out of the heart proceed evil thoughts, murders, adulteries, fornications, thefts, false witness, blasphemies" (Matthew 15:19). The first step toward seeing God is admitting that my heart is sinful and that I cannot see God unless my heart is changed.

Can the heart be changed? "I will give them an heart to know me, that I am the Lord" (Jeremiah 24:7). "This is the covenant that I will make with them after those days, saith the Lord, I will put my laws into their hearts and in their minds will I write them; and their sins and iniquities will I remember no more" (Hebrews 10:16-17). Jesus called this experience being "born again" or "born from above" (John 3:1-7), and Peter described it as becoming "partakers of the divine nature" (2 Peter 1:4). A person is not changed from the outside in; he must be changed from the inside out!

Our two kings, David and Saul, illustrate this truth. When God called Saul, "God gave him another heart" (1 Samuel 10:9), and the beginning of his reign was successful. But then he disobeyed God in failing to wait for Samuel and in acting as the priest; and that was the end of his reign. "But now thy kingdom shall not continue," Samuel announced, "the Lord hath sought him a man *after his own heart*" (1 Samuel 13:14, italics added). Why? "The Lord looketh on the heart" (1 Samuel 16:7). David was that man after God's own heart, not because he was sinless, but because his heart was *single*. Saul was a double-minded man: he tried to fear the people and fear the Lord at the same time, and it could not be done. Saul worried about the outward appearance: "Honour me now, I pray thee, before the elders of my people, and before Israel" (1 Samuel 15:30). David sought no honor for himself but only for God. "Let the enemy persecute my soul, and take it," David prays in Psalm 7:5. "Yea, let him tread down my life upon the earth, and lay mine honour in the dust." He closes that prayer with his desire that God alone might be glorified: "I will praise the Lord according to his righteousness: and will sing praise to the name of the Lord most high" (Psalm 7:17).

You cannot read the Psalms without learning that David cultivated his heart, the inner man. "I will praise thee, O Lord, with my whole heart" (Psalm 9:1). "Let the words of my mouth, and the meditation of my heart, be acceptable in thy sight, O Lord, my strength, and my redeemer" (Psalm 19:14). "Examine me, O Lord, and prove me; try my reins and my heart" (Psalm 26:2). "When thou saidst, Seek ye my face; my heart said unto thee, Thy face, Lord, will I seek" (Psalm 27:8). "My heart trusted in him, and I am helped" (Psalm 28:7). "My heart is inditing [bubbling up with] a good matter: I speak of the things which I have made touching the king" (Psalm 45:1). (Did not Jesus say, "Out of the abundance of the heart the mouth speaketh" [Matthew 12:34]?) Psalm 57 records David's experiences in the cave when he was hiding from Saul, and twice he stated the desire of his heart: "Be thou exalted, O God, above the heavens; let thy glory be above all the earth" (vv. 5, 11).

What was David's secret? "My heart is fixed, O God, my heart is fixed: I will sing and give praise" (Psalm 57:7). Saul's heart was not fixed; it was divided and unstable. "A double minded man is unstable in all his ways" (James 1:8). Saul set his heart on receiving honor before the people, and he lost both that and the honor that comes only from God. David set his heart on God and sought to honor Him, and God honored him in a singular way. When the Lord told David that He would build him a house and give him a throne forever (a promise that Messiah would come from David's line), the king was overwhelmed. Like a child, David used his own name as he spoke to God: "What can David speak more to thee for the honour of thy servant? for thou knowest thy servant" (1 Chronicles 17:18).

The highest joy of man comes from cultivating the deepest part of man, the heart. When the heart is pure, then the vision is clear, and a man will see God.

What Is a "Pure Heart"?

The word that is translated "pure" has two basic meanings: "clean" and "unmixed." Our English word *cathartic* comes from this Greek word. A carthartic is an agent used by a doctor for the cleansing of the physical system. A psychiatrist also uses catharsis on the emotional level to "cleanse" the patient of hostilities and other destructive attitudes. There is also a spiritual catharsis, a cleansing of the inner man. "Purifying their hearts by faith" (Acts 15:9) is one example. "The blood of Jesus Christ his Son cleanseth us from all sin" (1 John 1:7) is another.

But the word as it is used in our Beatitude takes the second meaning; for being "pure in heart" involves being *unmixed* as well as being clean. Milk that is pure is not adulterated with water. Gold with the dross removed is pure gold. Wheat with the chaff removed is pure wheat. The basic idea is that of *integrity*, singleness of heart, as opposed to duplicity, a double heart, a divided heart. When God cleanses the sinner and makes him His child, He does more than merely wash away sin. He puts within him a new heart that wants to focus wholly on God. "I will give them one heart, and one way, that they may fear me for ever" (Jeremiah 32:39). This is spiritual and moral integrity.

It was this integrity that made David a successful king, and it was the lack of this integrity that corrupted and defeated Saul. God rejected Saul's kingship, but "He chose David also his servant, and took him from following the sheepfolds. . . . So he [David] fed them according to the integrity of his heart; and guided them by the skillfulness of his hands" (Psalm 78:70, 72). No matter how skillful the hands may be, if the heart is divided, the work will be destroyed. Samuel Johnson stated it beautifully: "Integrity without knowledge is weak and useless, and knowledge without integrity is dangerous and dreadful." Peter illustrates the first, and Judas the second. Peter loved Jesus Christ and boasted that he would die for Him; he had integrity but not knowledge. Judas knew where the Lord was, where He would pray, and what He could do; but he lacked integrity and used his knowledge to destroy himself and others.

Integrity of heart was a passionate concern of David, as is witnessed by many statements in the Psalms. "Judge me, O Lord, according to my righteousness, and according to mine integrity that is in me" (Psalm 7:8). "Let integrity and uprightness preserve me; for I wait on thee" (Psalm 25:21). "Judge me, O Lord, for I have walked in mine integrity. . . . But as for me, I will walk in mine integrity" (Psalm 26:1, 11). "As for me, thou upholdest me in mine integrity, and settest me before thy face for ever" (Psalm 41:12). That last verse is perhaps the closest thing to our Beatitude that you will find in the Psalms: David had a pure heart, and he saw the face of God.

This singleness of heart is illustrated by Jesus in Matthew 6:19-23, when He talks about the eye. This is in the section of the Sermon on the Mount dealing with our relationship to wealth, and He is warning us against being double-minded, trying to serve both God and money. "The light of the body is the eye: if therefore thine eye be single, thy whole body shall be full of light. But if thine eye be evil, thy whole body shall be full of darkness. If therefore the light that is in thee be darkness, how great is that darkness!" (Matthew 6:22-23). After illustrating this truth by means of the human body, Jesus then illustrates it again by means of human relationships. "No man can serve two masters" (Matthew 6:24). Jesus is speaking here about singleness of devotion, desire, and direction. Psalm 86:11 explains it: "Teach me thy way, O Lord; I will walk in thy truth: unite my heart to fear thy name." No man can ever hope to see God whose heart is divided between the Lord and the world.

Our relationship with God must be based on love. For our hearts to love anything other than God is to commit spiritual adultery. "Ye adulterers and adulteresses, know ye not that the friendship of the world is enmity with God? Whosoever therefore will be a friend of the world is the enemy of God" (James 4:4). Because men are at war with God, they are at war with each other. "Saul became David's enemy continually" (1 Samuel 18:29). The only cure for spiritual adultery is, "Draw nigh to God, and he will draw nigh to you. Cleanse your hands, ye sinners; and purify [make chaste] your hearts, ye double minded" (James 4:8). "Thou shalt love the Lord thy God with *all* thy heart" (Matthew 22:37, italics added). David did not have a *sinless* heart, but he did have a *single* heart; and that made him a man after God's own heart. "I have found David the son of Jesse, a man after mine own heart, which shall fulfill all my will" (Acts 13:22). This verse brings out the contrasts between Saul and David. Saul talked about God's will, but David fulfilled it. Saul wanted his own will, but David wanted God's will. And Saul obeyed only part of God's will, whereas David fulfilled all of it.

How do we maintain this priceless integrity of heart? *By being utterly honest with God, others, and ourselves; and by seeking to honor God alone.* When you read about the life of David, you see a man who sought to live openly and honestly. Twice in his life, David resorted to duplicity, and in both instances he got into trouble. The first occurred when David fled to Gath and tried to escape the sword of Saul by joining the ranks of the enemy. (Gath was originally the home of Goliath, you will recall.) It became clear that David was no safer in Gath than he was in Judah, so "he changed his behaviour before them, and feigned himself mad in their hands, and scrabbled on the doors of the gate, and let his spittle fall down upon his beard" (1 Samuel 21:13). This masquerade enabled David to escape, and one result of this experience was the conviction that faith in God alone is the secret of God's protection. David records this conviction in Psalm 34. Duplicity led David almost to death. He fled to the cave of Adullam, and there he wrote Psalm 57 and cried out: "My heart is fixed, O God, my heart is fixed!" No more duplicity.

David's second masquerade was following the sin with Bathsheba, when he pretended to honor her husband, Uriah. His ruse did not work, and he had to resort to outright murder. Psalm 51 is the record of that experience, and once again the integrity of the inner man comes to the fore. "Behold, thou desirest truth in the inward parts" (v. 6). "Create in me a clean heart, O God; and renew a right [steadfast, established] spirit within me" (v. 10). Certainly David had sinned against Bathsheba and Uriah, but when he considered his sin in relationship to the integrity of his heart, he had to pray, "Against thee, thee only, have I sinned, and done this evil in thy sight" (v. 4).

Saul's life, however, was one masquerade after another, climaxing in that visit to the witch's cave. "Saul disguised himself" announces the historian (1 Samuel 28:8), and from the human point of view, this was true. But from the spiritual point of view, Saul did not disguise himself: *he revealed himself.* In the integrity of his heart, David had fled to a cave and there found God's help. In the duplicity of his heart, Saul fled to a cave and discovered that God had forsaken him, and the masquerade was over.

It is instructive to contrast the death of David and the death of Saul; the one resting confidently and directing the affairs of his kingdom up to the very end; the other staggering out into the darkness of defeat and having no control over himself or his kingdom. Saul's last actions are identified with night: "Saul disguised himself, and put on other raiment, and he went, and two men with him, and they came to the woman by night. . . . And they rose up, and went away that night" (1 Samuel 28:8, 25). Like Judas centuries later, Saul went out, "and it was night" (John 13:30). But David's last days are identified with light. "Now these be the last words of David. . . . He that ruleth over men must be just, ruling in the fear of God. And he shall be as the light of the morning, when the sun riseth, even a morning without clouds" (2 Samuel 23:1, 3-4).

When you read David's psalms, you realize that he was utterly honest before God. He never prayed anything that he did not mean. If he was afraid or sick or discour-

126 Live Like a King

aged, he admitted it. Psalm 142 is one of his "cave songs," and in it he says, "I poured out my complaint before him; I shewed before him my trouble. When my spirit was overwhelmed within me, then thou knewest my path" (vv. 2-3). Imagine complaining to God! "Attend unto me," David cries in Psalm 55:2, "and hear me: I mourn in my complaint, and make a noise." He was honest with God in his living and in his praying, and this maintained his integrity. He was a man after God's own heart.

The person who, like the Pharisees, pretends to be holy and tries to serve two masters, eventually becomes shallow and hollow. His is a surface religion that never reaches the heart. He has to use so much energy acting out a part that he has no strength left to live. There is no substitute for integrity. "Blessed are the pure in heart."

How Do We "See God"?

"For they shall see God." This is the highest blessing possible to man, for when you see God, you see Him who is (as the theologians put it) "the Source, Support, and End of all things." Since nothing is higher than God, then seeing God must be the highest joy that we can experience. It was this joy that motivated and excited men and women in Bible days and also inspired the great saints of church history. Moses prayed, "I beseech thee, shew me thy glory" (Exodus 33:18). David wrote his heart's desire in Psalm 42:1-2: "As the hart panteth after the water brooks, so panteth my soul after thee, O God. My soul thirsteth for God, for the living God: when shall I come and appear before God?" Phillip said to Jesus, "Show us the Father, and it is enough for us" (John 14:8, NASB). Of course it was for this purpose that Jesus came, that He might reveal God to us. "He that hath seen me hath seen the Father" (John 14:9).

Why do we seem to have so little of this hunger for God in the church today? We are not lacking in programs or people, activities or "results"; but we are lacking in a vision of God or even a desire for such a vision. The men and women God has used in past days have been characterized by a deep hunger to see God and know Him intimately. They have echoed the prayer of David, "O God, thou art my God; early will I seek thee: my soul thirsteth for thee, my flesh longeth for thee in a dry and thirsty land, where no water is; to see thy power and thy glory, so as I have seen thee in the sanctuary" (Psalm 63:1-2). If Isaiah's experience is any pattern, it would seem that *seeing* God is a condition for *serving* God. "In the year that king Uzziah died, I saw also the Lord sitting upon a throne, high and lifted up, and his train filled the temple" (Isaiah 6:1). This was also Paul's experience: he saw a light, and then he saw the Lord.

There is a sense, of course, in which God cannot be seen. "No man hath seen God at any time" (John 1:18). Even Moses was unable to look upon God in His very essence. "Thou canst not see my face," the Lord told him, "for there shall no man see me, and live" (Exodus 33:20). Paul, who visited the third heaven, described God as the One "who only hath immortality, dwelling in the light which no man can approach unto; whom no man hath seen, nor can see" (1 Timothy 6:16). Just as the human eye is blinded—and possibly destroyed—by gazing at the full light of the sun, so the spiritual eye cannot behold God in His fullness. No wonder Moses hid his face at the burning bush, "for he was afraid to look upon God" (Exodus 3:6).

We need that sense of respect today, for too many of God's people evidence a flippant familiarity with God that is not only disrespectful but outright disgusting. They know God in a secondhand way, but they want us to believe they are among His intimates. They have not yet had the deep experience of Job: "I have heard of thee by the hearing of the ear: but now mine eye seeth thee. Wherefore I abhor myself, and repent in dust and ashes" (Job 42:5-6). The apostle John, an intimate friend of Jesus, had a similar experience: "When I saw him, I fell at his feet as dead" (Revelation 1:17).

No, God in His essence cannot be seen. How, then, do we see God? When the heart is pure, then the eyes are opened to the vision of God wherever He may appear. To be sure, ultimately the children of God will in heaven "see his face" (Revelation 22:4). But it is not this final "beatific vision" of the saints and mystics that our Beatitude is talking about. Jesus is promising us the vision of God here and now. It is a basic principle that we see what we love; so if our hearts are united to fear and love God, then we will see God. We will live in a world that is filled with God!

To begin with, we will see God in His creation. "The heavens declare the glory of God, and the firmament sheweth his handiwork" (Psalm 19:1). The Psalms are filled with expressions of joy and wonder as the writer looked at God's world and saw God Himself. In Psalm 29, for example, David watched a storm as it swept over the mountains; but he did not simply see a storm: *he saw God.* The thunder was the voice of the Lord, and the rushing waters were the throne of the Lord! Instead of showing fear as he saw the trees breaking under the wind and the rivers rising, David shouted with confidence, "The Lord sitteth upon the flood; yea, the Lord sitteth King for ever!" (Psalm 29:10). Because David had a pure heart, he saw God in the stars and in the storms, and he enjoyed living in God's world.

The Lord Jesus had the same vision of God. He saw the providence of God in the fall of the sparrow and the generosity of God in the beauty of the lily. He watched a farmer sow his seed and in that saw the Word of God planted in men's hearts. When the sun came up Jesus beheld the grace of God: "for he maketh his sun to rise on the evil and on the good" (Matthew 5:45). Likewise, the rain reminded Him that the Father "sendeth rain on the just and on the unjust" (Matthew 5:45). For Jesus, nature was alive with God! Not a nebulous Something, a First Cause, or a Prime Mover—but a heavenly Father. "This is my Father's world!"

True, there is sin in it, and with sin comes sorrow and death. "For we know that the whole creation groans and suffers the pains of childbirth together unto now" (Romans 8:22, NASB). But in spite of what sin has done and what sinners are now doing, this is still God's creation, and His fingerprints and footprints are clearly seen by the saint who has a pure heart. Whenever I become disgusted at the civilization men have built, I look deeply into the creation God has built; I read Psalm 104 and give thanks.

We see God in creation, but we also see God in circumstances. In Psalms 105 and 106, for example, the writer saw the hand of God in the history of His people. A. T. Pierson used to say, "History is His story"—and he was right. When Matthew wrote his gospel, he used the word *fulfilled* at least a dozen times, showing us that the events in the life of Christ were controlled by the hand of God. His birth was the fulfillment of Isaiah 7:14; His flight to Egypt fulfilled Hosea 11:1; His growing up in Nazareth fulfilled the promise in the prophets, "He shall be called a Nazarene" (a rejected one). Our Lord's miracles of healing fulfilled Isaiah 53:4. Over and over in the gospel of Matthew we are told that our Lord's earthly life was a plan from God. And if you and I are in the will of God—if our hearts are single—we too shall see God in the circumstances of life. This was Paul's conviction when he wrote Romans 8:28: "We know that all things work together for good to them that love God, to them who are the called according to his purpose."

Psalm 23 makes clear that David saw God in the circumstances of his life. Life was not a series of accidents; it was a series of appointments. The Shepherd was in control. Even when David strayed and circumstances were painful, he still saw the Shepherd restoring him and refreshing him. When David looked back he saw God: "Surely goodness and mercy shall follow me all the days of my life"; and when he looked ahead he saw God: "I will dwell in the house of the Lord forever" (Psalm 23:6). Even when going through the dark valley David saw God: "For thou art with me." It is significant that in verse 4 David changes from the third person *he* to the second person *thou.*

We see God not only in the circumstances of our own lives but in the march of events in the world. Thoreau was once asked if he wanted to read the newspaper, and he replied that he had read one once! "Blessed are they who never read a newspaper," wrote Thoreau, "for they shall see Nature, and, through her, God." But why sacrifice one for the other? I believe it was John Wesley who said that he read the newspaper to see what God was doing in His world. There is no such thing as "secular" and "sacred" to the person with a pure heart and a single eye. "Who can utter the mighty acts of the Lord?" asks the writer of Psalm 106, whose eye penetrated deep into the mysteries of God's ways in the world. Nature and life are windows through which we should see God, but if we lack that integrity of heart they become mirrors in which we see only ourselves. Jesus taught this in His parable of the foolish farmer (Luke 12:13-21). In his bumper crop and sudden wealth, the farmer did not see God: he saw only himself. Count the eleven personal pronouns in the farmer's soliloquy, and note the repetition of "I will." This man was not pure in heart. He did not see God; he saw only himself.

The pure in heart see God in creation and circumstances and also in His Word. Unlike any other book, the Bible demands preparation of heart if its message is to be understood. As Phillips Brooks put it, "Obedience is the organ of spiritual knowledge." He finds his basis for this statement in John 7:17: "If any man is willing to do his will, he shall know of the teaching, whether it is of God, or whether I speak from myself" (NASB). We do not understand and then obey: that is instruction. We obey by faith, and then we understand: that is illumination. The double-minded man will never see God in the Bible. He may be book-taught and man-taught, but he will never be God-taught. His mind may grasp facts, but his heart will never lay hold of truths. The Pharisees knew the traditions of the fathers and the opinions of the scholars, but they did not know God. And He was right there in their midst! Bible study is good and important, but Bible knowledge should lead to a deeper knowledge of God. "You search the Scriptures, because you think that in them you have eternal life; and it is these that bear witness of Me" (John 5:39, NASB).

THE WIDER VISION

The experience of seeing God through the eyes of the heart is not a momentary thing; it is constant and growing. "But we all, with unveiled face beholding as in a mirror the glory of the Lord, are being transformed into the same image, from glory to glory, even as by the Spirit of the Lord" (2 Corinthians 3:18, literal translation). The pure in heart have nothing to hide, nothing to defend, nothing to explain. Their faces are unveiled. They advance "from glory to glory" until that day when they see Christ and become eternally like Him.

When you start to see God, you also start to see what God sees. You begin to see yourself in the light of God's glory. Abraham stood and talked with the Lord and called himself "but dust and ashes" (Genesis 18:27). Job saw God and said, "I abhor myself, and repent in dust and ashes" (Job 42:6). Peter fell down at Jesus' feet and said, "Depart from me; for I am a sinful man, O Lord" (Luke 5:8). Paul saw himself as "less than the least of all saints" (Ephesians 3:8) and the chief of sinners (1 Timothy 1:15). The vision of God humbles a man. "Therefore I was left alone, and saw this great vision," wrote Daniel (10:8), "and there remained no strength in me: for my comeliness was turned in me into corruption, and I retained no strength." Spiritual sight leads to spiritual insight. Isaiah saw the Lord and cried, "Woe is me! for I am undone" (Isaiah 6:5).

You not only see yourself in a new light, but you also see others in a new light. When the scribes and Pharisees looked at the publicans and sinners, they saw them as rebels; but Jesus saw them as lost coins, lost sheep, and lost sons. The Pharisees saw God as a Judge to condemn these rebels, but Jesus saw God as a seeking Shepherd and a waiting Father. The Pharisees saw Jesus as a glutton and a drunk, the friend of publicans and sinners. Jesus saw Himself as a Physician who had come to heal the brokenhearted. It is impossible to divorce our vision of God and our insight into ourselves and others. If we would know each other, we must first know God.

The eyes see what the heart loves. If the heart loves God and is single in this devotion, then the eyes will see God whether others see Him or not. Nothing robs the heart of spiritual vision like sin. Saul's repeated disobedience blinded him to God, circumstances, Samuel, and David. Saul treated his enemies like friends and his friends like enemies. No wonder Paul prayed that the "eyes" of our understanding might be enlightened (Ephesians 1:18). Literally, it is "the eyes of your heart." Physically, our eyes tend to deteriorate; but spiritually, our eyes ought to become keener and the vision brighter. If the light enters the body through the eyes, and the "windows of the heart" become soiled, then the light grows dimmer and dimmer. Then we have to pray, with David, "Wash me!" (Psalm 51:7).

The most important part of your life is the part only God sees. He knows whether or not your heart is pure. He wants your heart to be pure, for only then can you see God and, in seeing God, receive all that He has and enjoy all that He is.

Blessed are the peacemakers: for they shall be called the children of God.

(Matthew 5:9)

The work of righteousness shall be peace; and the effect of righteousness quietness and assurance forever.

(Isaiah 32:17)

For the wisdom that is from above is first pure, then peaceable, gentle, and easy to be intreated, full of mercy and good fruits, without partiality, and without hypocrisy.

(James 3:17)

Behold, how good and how pleasant it is for brethren to dwell together in unity!

(Psalm 133:1)

Let the peace of God rule in your hearts.

(Colossians 3:15)

But the fruit of the Spirit is love, joy, peace.

(Galatians 5:22)

9

The Peacemakers

The Bible is a book about peace. There are nearly four hundred references to peace in its pages, either personal peace with God or peace among men on an individual or a national level. The Bible opens with peace and closes with peace; and the reason there is war in-between is because of the opposition of Satan and the disobedience of man. God is not at war with the world, but the world is at war with God.

We must bear in mind that peace in the Bible is much more than the absence of war. There is no strife in a cemetery, but one would hardly use a cemetery as an example of peace. In the Bible, peace is a positive force; it signifies the presence of all that is good and wonderful. When two Jews meet each other or part from each other, they say, "Shalom! Peace!" but they mean much more than, "May you have no battles!" The word *shalom* contains in it a desire for all of the goodness that God can give, a total well-being for mind and heart and body. Peace is a creative force, and a peacemaker is a person who releases this creative force to change his world.

If you and I are to be peacemakers in a world filled with strife, then we must understand four basic truths about peace.

THE ORIGIN OF PEACE

The first truth is this: the source of peace is God. Six times in the New Testament He is called "the God of Peace." He is the God of peace as far as His person is concerned; there are no conflicts in the nature of God. You and I have battles within because we have a higher and a lower nature, but that is not so with God. His person is at perfect peace; His attributes harmoniously dwell and work together. God is at perfect peace with Himself. That is why He is called the God of peace. One of the great Old Testament names for God is "Jehovah-shalom"—"the Lord is our peace" (Judges 6:24).

Not only is He the God of peace as far as His person and His nature are concerned, but He is the God of peace as far as His will is concerned. "For I know the thoughts that I think toward you, saith the Lord, thoughts of peace, and not of evil, to give you an expected end" (Jeremiah 29:11). God thinks about us; that in itself is a miracle! And the thoughts—the plans—that He thinks are for our peace, to accomplish a perfect purpose for our lives. The enemy would have us believe that God never thinks about us, or that His thoughts are dangerous and painful. But such is not the case. God does think about us, and His thoughts point to peace.

He is the God of peace in the outworking of His will. Critics tell us that the Old Testament is certainly not a revelation of God, because its pages are filled with war and judgment. But if you read the Old Testament carefully, you discover that God's working is first peace, then war. The account of human history begins with peace, and it was only when man sinned and joined with the enemy that God declared war. But even in His declaration of war there is the message of peace, the promise of the coming Redeemer (Genesis 3:15). The law of war that God gave to Israel in Deuteronomy 20 makes clear that Israel was to declare peace before it declared war. If the city refused to accept terms of peace, then Israel had to fight.

This same principle was followed by our Lord Jesus Christ, the Prince of Peace. At His birth, the angel announced "on earth peace, good will toward men" (Luke 2:14). There could have been peace on earth, had men received Him; but they said, "We will not have this man to reign over us!" (Luke 19:14).

How did Jesus respond to man's rejection of peace? "Suppose ye that I am come to give peace on earth? I tell you, Nay; but rather division" (Luke 12:51). On that day when He rode into Jerusalem ("city of peace") and fulfilled the Old Testament prophecy, the city still would not receive Him. That was why He wept over the city, saying, "If thou hadst known, even thou, at least in this thy day, the things which belong unto thy peace! But now they are hid from thine eyes" (Luke 19:42). There was certainly no peace on earth!

Was there peace any place? Yes! The whole multitude of disciples rejoiced and praised God, saying, "Blessed be the King that cometh in the name of the Lord: peace in heaven, and glory in the highest" (Luke 19:38). Peace in heaven! There is no peace on earth, but there is peace in heaven—and that peace can be experienced on earth in the hearts of those who will yield to Christ.

Jesus Christ is God's Peacemaker. "For he is our peace," wrote Paul in Ephesians 2:14, referring to Christ's work of uniting believing Jews and Gentiles into one body, the church. He made peace by His sacrificial death on the cross; and He preaches peace through His Spirit in the world today (Ephesians 2:15, 17). As He faced the tortures of Calvary, Jesus was able to say to His disciples, "Peace I leave with you, my peace I give unto you" (John 14:27). "These things have I spoken unto you, that in me ye might have peace" (John 16:33).

Our God is the God of peace, and our Savior is the Prince of Peace. The Holy Spirit is the Spirit of peace, for it is He that applies and supplies the peace of God in our lives. "But the fruit of the Spirit is love, joy, peace" (Galatians 5:22). The source of peace is God; there is no other source. If you and I are going to be peacemakers, we must know God and draw upon His supply of peace.

THE OPPOSITION TO PEACE

The enemy of peace is sin. This is the second truth that the believer must lay hold of if he is going to be a peacemaker; otherwise he will misunderstand what happens when people reject his peace. Jesus Christ is the Prince of Peace, yet three times in John's gospel we are told that there was a division because of Him (7:43; 9:16; 10:19). "He stirreth up the people" was one of the accusations at His trial (Luke 23:5). The apostle Paul was God's ambassador of peace, yet men said of him, "We have found this man a pestilent fellow!" (Acts 24:5). Isaiah 32:17 promises, "The work of righteousness shall be peace," but it seems that those who "hunger and thirst after righteousness" sometimes are the cause of war! "Yea, and all that will live godly in Christ Jesus shall suffer persecution" (2 Timothy 3:12).

According to James 4:1-4, there are three wars going on in our world today.

> From whence come wars and fightings among you? come they not hence, even of your lusts that war in your members? Ye lust, and have not: ye kill, and desire to have, and cannot obtain: ye fight and war, yet ye

sire to have, and cannot obtain: ye fight and war, yet ye have not, because ye ask not. You ask, and receive not, because ye ask amiss, that ye may consume it upon your lusts. Ye adulterers and adulteresses, know ye not that the friendship of the world is enmity with God? whosoever therefore will be a friend of the world is the enemy of God.

People are at war with each other because they are at war with themselves ("your lusts that war in your members"); and they are at war with themselves because they are at war with God. God has His enemies: the world (v. 4), the flesh (v. 1), and the devil (v. 7); and whoever sides with these enemies declares war on God. Whenever you declare war on God, you become a troublemaker, not a peacemaker.

This helps to explain why so much trouble results when a Christian gets out of the will of God. Abraham tried to escape the famine in Canaan by going to Egypt; and there he created so many problems that the ruler had to ask him to leave (Genesis 12). Lot fell in love with Sodom, and the result was a conflict between him and Abraham (Genesis 13). David committed adultery with Bathsheba and brought tragic discipline down upon both his family and the nation. Jonah disobeyed God and created a storm that almost wrecked the ship and sent an unsaved, pagan crew out into a lost eternity. A believer living in sin is a great troublemaker, because sin is the enemy of peace.

At the same time, a believer living a godly life can be a cause of trouble. Why? Because a peacemaker reveals the war that is going on in the lives of unsaved people. Stephen's calmness as he faced his accusers only incited their hatred all the more. "I am for peace: but when I speak, they are for war" (Psalm 120:7). It has often been said that wherever Paul went, the result was either a revival or a riot, and sometimes it was both! "These that have

turned the world upside down are come hither also!"
(Acts 17:6). As long as men's hearts are sinful, there is
going to be war in the world. The only solution is righteousness.

This explains why "Blessed are the pure in heart"
precedes "Blessed are the peacemakers." Only the pure
in heart can be peacemakers. "The work of righteousness
shall be peace; and the effect of righteousness quietness
and assurance forever" (Isaiah 32:17). "But the wisdom
that is from above is first pure, then peaceable. . . . And
the fruit of righteousness is sown in peace of them that
make peace" (James 3:17a-18). If I am at war with God
because there is sin in my life, then I cannot be a peacemaker. It was Abraham who made peace, not Lot. Lot
was a friend of the world and therefore the enemy of
God, whereas Abraham was a friend of God and therefore the enemy of the world. Abraham sowed peace, and
his descendants have been a channel of peace in the
world. Lot sowed sin, and his descendants (the Ammon-
ites and the Moabites, Genesis 19:36-38) were the enemies of Israel throughout history.

God's throne is a righteous throne, and His scepter is
a scepter of righteousness. If we are going to reign in life,
then we must deal with sin in our lives. Grace reigns
"through righteousness" (Romans 5:21). Jesus Christ is
"King of Righteousness" (Melchizedek) and "King of
Peace" (Salem). In Him, "righteousness and peace have
kissed each other" (Psalm 85:10). David was a man after
God's own heart and sought, in spite of his failures, to
have a righteous reign in obedience to God. Saul's throne
was a throne of deceit and disobedience. Saul's own son,
Jonathan, admitted, "My father hath troubled the land"
(1 Samuel 14:29). Even after Saul's death "there was a
long war between the house of Saul and the house of David" (2 Samuel 3:1) until all the tribes of Israel crowned
David their rightful king. These things are an allegory: un-

til Jesus Christ is crowned King in our lives and sin is put to death by the Spirit, we can never be peacemakers.

THE OUTFLOW OF PEACE

The source of peace is God, and the enemy of peace is sin. The third truth is: the minister of peace is the Christian. The angels can come and announce, "Peace on earth!" but they can never minister as peacemakers, simply because they have never personally experienced the peace of God. We have experienced it, and therefore we can share it. "For we ourselves also were sometimes foolish, disobedient, deceived, serving divers lusts and pleasures, living in malice and envy, hateful, and hating one another" (Titus 3:3). But we came to the cross where Jesus Christ made peace, and there we found forgiveness for our sins. "Therefore being justified by faith, we have peace with God through our Lord Jesus Christ" (Romans 5:1). The war is now over; and because we are no longer at war with God, we are no longer at war with ourselves. The "peace of God, which passeth all understanding" (Philippians 4:7) moves into our hearts and minds, and we are at peace with ourselves. Having received peace with God and having experienced the peace of God, we are now ready to be peacemakers. We are reigning in life because the peace of God is ruling in our hearts (Colossians 3:15).

We begin this ministry of peace by making peace with our brother, and this starts with controlling anger (Matthew 5:21-26). Hatred in the heart is the equivalent of murder, and it begins with anger. More important than bringing a gift to the altar is getting right with my brother so I can bring my gift with a heart that is right with God. Worship and warfare cannot exist at the same altar. "Agree with thine adversary quickly" (Matthew 5:25) does not suggest cowardice or compromise. Rather, it suggests that we start with the positive before we deal with the negative; it means finding where I *agree* with my brother before I discuss our areas of disagreement. When there is war in my heart, I always look for points of difference; but when there is peace in my heart, I always look for points of agreement.

In the early years of my ministry, whenever anyone approached me with criticism, I usually lit into him and tried to change his mind. Then I learned to agree with my critics quickly, to find someplace where we could stand together, and then from that place move into a constructive discussion of the problem. The words "Yes, I agree with you that—" have a way of disarming people and softening the blow. If you are out to win an argument, you will never agree with your adversary; but if you are out to *win a brother,* you will begin by declaring peace and not war.

Our Lord amplifies this matter in Matthew 18:15-17, where He instructs us to visit the estranged brother privately and to seek to win him back. If this fails, then take one or two others with you; and if that fails, it is necessary to take it to the church. The lesson is obvious: the longer a man delays in dealing with sin, the larger the influence of that sin grows. First, the sin involves only two people; then four are involved; and then the whole assembly of believers! "A brother offended is harder to be won than a strong city" (Proverbs 18:19). But Proverbs 16:32 tells us, "He that is slow to anger is better than the mighty; and he that ruleth his spirit than he that taketh a city." If I am reigning in life through Christ and if I have His peace within, then I can storm the city and win the battle in love!

As peacemakers, we are also to seek to bring peace to our enemies. The instructions in Matthew 5:38-48 are both demanding and disturbing. Certainly the Lord was not giving a set of rules to follow on every occasion; otherwise He was contradicting other admonitions in Scripture. It seems that He was describing *an attitude of heart* that is willing to suffer pain and loss if it will lead to the winning of an enemy. At least this is the interpretation Paul gave to the passage: "Dearly beloved, avenge not yourselves, but rather give place unto wrath: for it is written, Vengeance is mine; I will repay, saith the Lord. Therefore if thine enemy hunger, feed him; if he thirst, give him drink: for in so doing thou shalt heap coals of fire on his head. Be not overcome of evil, but overcome evil with good" (Romans 12:19-21). Whatever rules my life, I will try to use to rule the lives of others; and, whatever I use to control others will ultimately control me. To be sure, I may not be able to win every brother or convert every enemy. "If it be possible, as much as lieth in you, live peaceably with all men" (Romans 12:18). Sometimes it is not possible. But we must not give up too soon.

As peacemakers, we must never compromise just to bring about peace. "Peace at any price" is never right in the life of the believer. Peace at the expense of honesty and humility will only lead to more war. The quieting of the surface when the depths are still stormy is no lasting solution to the problem. "They have healed also the hurt of the daughter of my people slightly, saying, Peace, peace; when there is no peace" (Jeremiah 6:14). The false prophets in Ezekiel's day whitewashed the tottering walls and pretended that the situation was in safe hands. "Because, even because they have seduced my people, saying, Peace; and there was no peace; and one built up a wall, and, lo, others daubed it with untempered mortar" (Ezekiel 13:10). A false peace is more dangerous than an open war, because the problems have only been covered over. It is honesty, not hypocrisy, that makes for peace. "But the wisdom that is from above is first pure, then peaceable" (James 3:17).

Calvary is the greatest example of making peace. On the cross, God openly admitted the fact of sin. The horror of sin was not glossed over when Jesus died for the sins of the world. Instead of hiding sin, the Lord openly exposed it. *But then He suffered for sin.* And because of His sacrifice we are forgiven, and we can be forgiving. We need never fear to deal with sin, because it has already been dealt with at Calvary. The cross was His throne, and Jesus reigned as King when He made peace by the blood of His cross. His scepter had been a reed, and His crown was made of thorns; but He reigned, just the same. As believers, we, too, reign in life whenever we honestly and humbly deal with sin as we seek to win our brother or our enemy.

There is a price to pay. Is it worth it?

THE OUTCOME OF PEACE

Yes, it is worth it; for *the blessing of peace is godliness:* "they shall be called the children of God." The Father is the great Peacemaker; and when you and I become peacemakers, we become like our Father. Beginning with the fifth Beatitude, the blessings received are nothing less than attributes of God: merciful, pure in heart, peacemakers. Children are like their parents, and as peacemakers, we become more like the Father in heaven.

This fact is certainly illustrated in the lives of Saul and David. As time passed, Saul became more and more of a troublemaker, and David did all he could to bring about peace. On two occasions, David could have killed Saul; but David knew that this was not the way to deal with an enemy. In fact, when David even cut off a part of Saul's robe, his heart "smote him" (1 Samuel 24:5), so sensitive was he to God's will. When one of David's men urged him to kill Saul, David replied, "As the Lord liveth, the Lord shall smite him; or his day shall come to die; or he shall descend into battle, and perish" (1 Samuel 26:10). David knew that vengeance belongs to God. Because the peace of God controlled David's heart, the power of God controlled David's hand, and he did not use either the sword or the spear to destroy his enemy.

If any man was transformed from a troublemaker into a peacemaker, it was Saul of Tarsus. The very air that he breathed was "threatenings and slaughter" (Acts 9:1)! He knew the law, but the law could neither change him nor control him. When he saw Stephen die with glory on his face and a prayer of forgiveness on his lips, Saul never forgot it. Years later, he told that hushed Jewish crowd in the Temple, "When the blood of thy martyr Stephen was shed, I also was standing by, and consenting unto his death, and kept the raiment of them that slew him" (Acts 22:20). Saul of Tarsus the slave beheld Stephen the king, reigning in life and reigning in death! (The name *Stephen* means "crown.")

But unlike his namesake, Saul of Tarsus admitted his need and one day fell to his face and yielded to Jesus Christ. Here are two Sauls from Benjamin, both of whom fell; yet for King Saul, his fall meant defeat and death, and for Saul of Tarsus it meant victory and life. In the years that followed his conversion, Saul, "who is Paul," became a minister of reconciliation and an ambassador of peace, and eventually he paid for his ministry with his life. But it was worth it all! For Paul came to know Christ and became more and more like Him, even though he saw himself as "less than the least of all saints" (Ephesians 3:8) and the chief of sinners (1 Timothy 1:15).

Hatred can never be conquered with hatred. Only love can conquer hatred. And when love declares war on hatred, the battle is always a difficult one. Love is like light and reveals the darkness in hearts. Love challenges the enemy to be a better man, and this often makes the conflict worse, because no man wants to admit that he is less than his enemy. The quiet calmness and pitying love of our Lord when they arrested and tried Him must have infuriated His enemies. The contrast between their brittle religious piety and IIis living, loving righteousness was too much for them, so they had to destroy Him. But a peacemaker cannot really be destroyed, because the source of peace is God, and God is eternal. Jesus Christ arose from the dead, and today He shares His peace with all who will "kiss the Son" (Psalm 2:12) and trust in Him.

David and Solomon illustrate two aspects of this matter of peace. David was a man of war, because peace is not purchased cheaply. Solomon was a man of peace, and under his reign Israel reached its greatest heights of glory and prosperity. But Solomon built upon the victories his father had won. Jesus Christ is the Prince of Peace, but He had to fight that awesome battle against sin by dying on the cross. "Having made peace through the blood of his cross, by him to reconcile all things unto himself" (Colossians 1:20). Solomon built the Temple because David won the battles, and in each we see the peace work of our Lord Jesus Christ.

As you and I seek to be peacemakers, men will treat us as they did Jesus. They will misunderstand us and not honestly seek for the truth. They will criticize us and accuse us. Eventually they will condemn us and crucify us. Hatred blinds, whereas love sharpens vision. Hatred looks for a victim, whereas love seeks a victory. The man of war throws stones, and the peacemaker builds a bridge out of those stones. The man of war comes with a sword, and the peacemaker disarms him with love and beats that sword into a plowshare. The man of war throws his spear, and the peacemaker beats it into a pruning hook. The peacemaker does not avoid the battle; instead, he transforms the battle into a ministry of reconciliation. How does he do this? Certainly not in his own strength! "The love of God is shed abroad in our hearts by the Holy Ghost which is given unto us" (Romans 5:5). "But the fruit of the Spirit is . . . peace" (Galatians 5:22).

*Blessed are they which are persecuted for righteousness'
sake, for theirs is the kingdom of heaven. Blessed are ye,
when men shall revile you, and persecute you, and shall
say all manner of evil against you falsely, for my sake. Rejoice, and be exceeding glad: for great is your reward in
heaven: for so persecuted they the prophets which were
before you.*

(Matthew 5:10-12)

*Woe unto you, when all men shall speak well of you! for
so did their fathers to the false prophets.*

(Luke 6:26)

*Beloved, think it not strange concerning the fiery trial
which is to try you, as though some strange thing happened unto you: but rejoice, inasmuch as ye are partakers
of Christ's sufferings; that, when his glory shall be revealed, ye may be glad also with exceeding joy.*

(1 Peter 4:12-13)

*They departed from the presence of the council, rejoicing
that they were counted worthy to suffer shame for his
name.*

(Acts 5:41)

If thou faint in the day of adversity, thy strength is small.

(Proverbs 24:10)

10

The Persecuted

There is a brand of Christianity today that seems unlike the kind that Jesus spoke about in the gospels and that Paul spoke about in the epistles. It is an easygoing, popular kind of religion that is acceptable to the world because it involves no conviction and no cross, or at least no cross as Jesus spoke of it. When He told the crowds that they had to take up a cross in order to be His disciples, the crowds left Him and eventually killed Him. The world has no problem accepting and following a religious leader who permits them to stay in their sins; but they will crucify the man who dares to point them to a narrow gate that leads to a narrow way. Even Peter was amazed that following Jesus involved a cross. "Be it far from thee, Lord: this shall not be unto thee" (Matthew 16:22).

I met a Christian friend one day whom I had not seen in several years, and he was telling me his experiences as a Christian. "By the way," he remarked, "the last time I heard you preach, you talked about Christians being persecuted. I'll have to confess to you that I don't agree with you. I have never been persecuted for being a Christian, and I don't believe it's a necessary part of the Christian life."

We had to part company just then, but had we remained together I would have pointed out to him that *the righteous have always suffered for their faith in one way or another.* It began with Abel's being killed by Cain—and Cain was a religious man, by the way. Moses chose "rather to suffer affliction with the people of God" (Hebrews 11:25) than to compromise in Egypt. Jesus Himself told us that the prophets were persecuted, and He warned His disciples that they, too, would be persecuted. The book of Acts and all of church history since then verify our Lord's prediction. 'Yea, and all that will live godly in Christ Jesus shall suffer persecution" (2 Timothy 3:12).

REASONS FOR PERSECUTION

The reasons for persecution are not difficult to understand. Jesus names two: we are persecuted "for righteousness' sake" and for His name's sake. We must be careful to distinguish between *persecution and punishment.* We are punished by good men for doing evil, and we are persecuted by bad men for doing good. Peter knew the difference: "If ye be reproached for the name of Christ, happy are ye. . . . But let none of you suffer as a murderer, or as a thief, or as an evildoer, or as a busybody in other men's matters. Yet if any man suffer as a Christian, let him not be ashamed; but let him glorify God on this behalf" (1 Peter 4:14-16).

Sad to say, some believers do not know the difference between being offensive and "the offense of the cross" (Galatians 5:11), or between being witnesses and being prosecuting attorneys. Jesus used the word *falsely,* and it is an important word. If I get into trouble because I talk too much or because I meddle or because I try to force my faith on other people, that is not persecution. If I am promoting my own cause and men reject me, that is not persecution. If I am arrogant and abusive in my attempt to witness for Christ and people want nothing to do with me, that is not persecution. But if I seek to do His will and honor His name and as a result I suffer, then that is persecution.

Some believers have an ego problem and want to be noticed and praised, so they deliberately get themselves into trouble in order to claim that they have been persecuted for the Lord. The Christian who is devotedly carrying his cross never has to manufacture persecution. If we live the way Jesus lived, then the world will treat us the way it treated Him, and we will share in "the fellowship of his sufferings" (Philippians 3:10).

True persecution comes "for righteousness' sake." It is the result of the believer's daring to live the Beatitudes. The world's philosophy is exactly opposite of that which Jesus expresses in the Beatitudes, and these opposite viewpoints lead to opposing ways of life. The narrow road that we walk is not parallel to the broad road: it runs right down the middle! We are walking in one direction, and the world is walking in the other, and it is impossible not to collide. Jesus tells us to be "poor in spirit," but the world tells us to build up our egos and be important. Humility is not a virtue that is admired in today's society. In fact, unbelievers look upon humility as a form of weakness. George Bernard Shaw stated their position perfectly when he said, "Leave it to the coward to make a religion of his cowardice by preaching humility."

Neither is the world interested in mourning over sin. Unbelievers will quickly regret the uncomfortable effects of sin, but even that passes away. Meekness they consider weakness, for, after all, it is the aggressive man who gets ahead in this world. "Winner take all, and the devil take the hindmost!" The world has no appetite for righteousness. Its motto is "Eat, drink, and be merry, for tomorrow we die!" Mercy—purity of heart—and peacemaking are concepts that are rarely, if ever, found in the mind of the unbeliever. To show mercy when your enemy is under your sword's point is to lose the victory. Such is "the counsel of the ungodly" (Psalm 1:1).

The root meaning of the word *righteousness* is "to divide, to be different." "If ye were of the world, the world would love his own: but because ye are not of the world, but I have chosen you out of the world, therefore the world hateth you" (John 15:19). The holy Son of God was a cause of division when He was in the world, and those who seek to live like Him will produce the same results. "If they have persecuted me," said Jesus, "they will also persecute you" (John 15:20b). Jesus was different, and a world that thrives on conformity cannot tolerate differences. We are children of light, and they are children of darkness. We are alive in the Spirit, and they are dead in sins. We live by faith, and they live by sight. We understand them, but they do not understand us.

We are persecuted "for righteousness' sake" and for His name's sake. "But all these things will they do unto you for my name's sake, because they know not him that sent me" (John 15:21). The Lord came to earth to reveal God's name to us (John 17:6). Because the world knows not God they know not His Son, Jesus Christ; ignorance always breeds suspicion, and suspicion breeds fear. Whatever a person fears, he attacks. That explains why sinful men killed God's Son and now try to kill those who have trusted Him. "For unto you it is given in the behalf of Christ, not only to believe on him, but also to suffer for his sake (Philippians 1:29). Let a man announce that he belongs to a religious group—be it Baptist, Presbyterian, Lutheran, or what have you—and few people, if anybody, will get upset. But let him announce that he is a Christian, let the name of Christ come into the conversation, and war is declared.

Persecution is a normal part of dedicated Christian living. It is not the thermostat of the Christian life: our love for Christ is that. But it is the thermometer; it helps us measure how much we are like the Savior.

RESPONSES TO PERSECUTION

As believers, we must *respond* to persecution and not *react*. We need to be prepared with the right attitude of mind. "Forasmuch then as Christ hath suffered for us in the flesh, arm yourselves likewise with the same mind" (1 Peter 4:1). A proper attitude of mind is a weapon in the battle against Satan. We do not react, then resent, and then retaliate. That is the way the world acts when difficulties come. No, the believer responds in a positive way, not because he seeks persecution, but because he expects it and is not surprised when it comes. Jesus tells us that there are three proper responses: we reign (Matthew 5:10), we rejoice (Matthew 5:12), and we release love (Matthew 5:43-48).

"For theirs is the kingdom of heaven" simply means that the believer reigns in life in the midst of persecution. He acts like a king, not a slave! The more King Saul persecuted David, the more David reigned in life through faith in God. David knew that he was the rightful king, for God had anointed David and promised him the throne. So he acted like a king! When he could have killed Saul, David exercised self-control and let him go free. When David could have slain Shimei for his stones and slanders, David ignored the man and left the matter with God. When you know you are a king, it is beneath your dignity to retaliate, because that only makes you like other people.

On March 11, 1830, a British girl was doing her lessons with her tutor, and the lesson that day had to do with the royal family. As she studied the genealogical chart in the book, she became aware of the astounding fact that she was next in line for the throne! At first she wept, and then she looked at her tutor and said, "I will be good!" The fact that little Victoria would one day be queen motivated her to live on a higher level; and the fact that you and I are already kings should motivate us not to retaliate.

After all, there are only three levels on which we can live: the demonic, the human, and the divine. Satan returns evil for good; men return good for good and evil for evil; but God returns good for evil. "He maketh his sun to rise on the evil and on the good, and sendeth rain on the just and on the unjust" (Matthew 5:45). People with low self-esteem quickly react and retaliate, because they must defend themselves. But believers who know they are kings are so filled with God's riches that it is beneath their dignity to retaliate. Jesus could have summoned legions of angels, yet He willingly let sinful men slap Him in the face, spit upon Him, pluck out His beard, mock Him, and then crucify Him.

Our first response is to reign, and our second is to rejoice: "Rejoice, and be exceeding glad" (Matthew 5:12). Impossible? The disciples did it when they were persecuted: "They departed from the presence of the council, rejoicing that they were counted worthy to suffer shame for his name" (Acts 5:41). Years later, Peter wrote: "If ye be reproached for the name of Christ, happy are ye" (1 Peter 4:14). How is it possible for suffering people to rejoice? To begin with, we realize that it is a privilege to be persecuted for Jesus sake. The very persecution is evidence that we are living like Him and glorifying Him, and that ought to make any Christian rejoice. "The fellowship of his sufferings" (Philippians 3:10) is the closest fellowship possible: when we are in the furnace, the Son of God is there with us.

But something else makes us rejoice: we have new opportunities to witness for Christ. Our English word *martyr* is a transliteration of the Greek word that means "witness." Stephen suffered persecution, even unto death, and one result was the conversion of Saul of Tarsus. When the world sees a godly believer rejoice in persecution, it realizes that the Christian life is something more than a mere religion. The greatest opportunities we have for witnessing come when the stones are flying.

Persecution also gives us an opportunity to grow. When the world praises us, we are in spiritual danger; but when the world persecutes us, we can be sure we are living for Christ and becoming more like Him. The furnace of suffering purges out the dross of sin. "For he that hath suffered in the flesh hath ceased from sin; that he no longer should live the rest of his time in the flesh to the lusts of men, but to the will of God" (1 Peter 4:1*b*-2). Persecution has a way of driving us to God; it helps us examine our priorities and strengthen our spiritual roots. Suffering by itself never makes a man grow; but suffering in the will of God and for the glory of God is a great stimulus to spiritual development. "Before I was afflicted I went astray: but now have I kept thy word. . . . It is good for me that I have been afflicted; that I might learn thy statutes" (Psalm 119:67, 71).

This spiritual joy, of course, is not something that we work up; it is the gift of the Holy Spirit: "for the Spirit of glory and of God resteth upon you" (1 Peter 4:14). This joy comes from trusting and loving Christ. "Whom having not seen, ye love; in whom, though now ye see him not, yet believing, ye rejoice with joy unspeakable and full of glory" (1 Peter 1:8). Even our Lord Jesus endured the cross because of "the joy that was set before him" (Hebrews 12:2).

We respond to persecution by reigning, rejoicing, and releasing love. "Love your enemies, bless them that curse you, do good to them that hate you, and pray for

them which despitefully use you, and persecute you"
(Matthew 5:44). This is the consequence of reigning and
rejoicing.

Christian love is not a shallow sentiment; it is a settled attitude of the mind and heart that leads to definite
actions of the will. Christian love means that I treat you
the way God treats me. This is why Jesus adds to His com-
mand to love our enemies, "that ye may be the children of
your Father which is in heaven" (Matthew 5:45). God
loved us when we were His enemies, and He sent His Son
to die for us. We should treat our enemies the way God
has treated us—we should be patient, forgiving, and willing to sacrifice for their good, even though they may not
deserve it.

If we have sincere Christian love, it will reveal itself
in our prayers and our actions. We will pray for our enemies that they might come to know the Lord—not so that
our way will be easier, but so that *their* way will be easier.
We need the kind of love Jesus showed when He prayed,
"Father, forgive them; for they know not what they do"
(Luke 23:34). We need the kind of love Stephen showed
when he prayed, "Lord Jesus, receive my spirit. . . . Lord,
lay not this sin to their charge" (Acts 7:59-60). We do *not*
need to pray that fire from heaven will consume our enemies (Luke 9:54-56)!

But it is not enough to live and pray; we must act. By
doing something positive for our enemy, we release God's
love to touch his life. This is what Paul meant by "heaping
coals of fire on his head" (Romans 12:17-21). Our motives
may be questioned and our ministries rejected, but *for
Jesus' sake* we must do good to our enemies if ever they
are going to experience the grace of God and become
Christians. And even if they do not become Christians, we
become better Christians for having done the will of God.

REWARDS OF PERSECUTION

There are definite rewards for the believer who suffers persecution in the will of God. Some people may believe that rewards are a poor motive for obedience, but Jesus did not think so. To be sure, character is reward enough; but in His grace, Jesus was willing to add something extra. And, after all, whatever rewards we receive only bring greater glory to Him, both here and hereafter.

There is a present reward stated: "for theirs is the kingdom of heaven" (Matthew 5:10). He was not talking about *entering* the kingdom, because that is covered in the first Beatitude. He was talking about *enjoying* the kingdom. When you are able to exercise self-control in the midst of persecution and pray for your persecutors and do good to them, then you have entered into the secrets of the throne and the riches of His glory. No matter how little we may have of material things, we enjoy God's spiritual riches as we reign in life through Jesus Christ. To be sure, there is a future reward, and the Lord names it; but right here and now, we live like kings.

Another reward is our identification with Christ and the prophets: "for so persecuted they the prophets which were before you" (Matthew 5:12). What a holy band of saints to belong to! Here were believers "of whom the world was not worthy" (Hebrews 11:38), and we are privileged to fellowship with them. A man's company is a great revealer of a man's character. "Being let go, they went to their own company" (Acts 4:23). While He was ministering on earth, Jesus was identified with the suffering prophets of old. "Some say that thou art John the Baptist: some, Elias; and others, Jeremias, or one of the prophets" (Matthew 16:14). All three of the men named were persecuted because of their faith and their faithfulness.

Today we can enter into the riches of the kingdom and the fellowship of the martyrs; but there is also a future reward: "for great is your reward in heaven" (Matthew 5:12). Never minimize the present power of a future reward. Moses turned his back on Egypt and suffered for it because "he had respect unto the recompense of the reward" (Hebrews 11:26). Abraham walked by faith as he looked for that city God had promised him. Jesus encourages us today by promising us heavenly rewards tomorrow, and there is nothing wrong with this encouragement. "If we suffer, we shall also reign with him" (2 Timothy 2:12). One of the repeated themes of 1 Peter is suffering and glory; Peter wrote to encourage Christians going through fiery trials. It is easy for the comfortable saint to despise promised rewards; but let him go into the fires, and he might change his mind.

This is the last of the Beatitudes, the climax of them all. It is difficult to believe that men would persecute people who are humble and meek, who are seeking after righteousness, who are merciful and trying to make peace. But they do. The dedication of the saints only magnifies the depravity of the sinners.

The world welcomes a compromising Christian, but it hates the Christian who does the will of God. In some respects, this final Beatitude is the measure of the others. As we are growing in Christian character, we will experience more conflict. It is impossible to have one without the other.

We are never really finished with the Beatitudes, because there are always new discoveries of our own hearts and of God's grace. We grow in grace as we grow in knowledge—knowledge of Christ and knowledge of ourselves. We reign in life, but there is always new territory to conquer and control. We enjoy the kingdom that we might enlarge the kingdom. Jesus dealt with this theme in His statement about salt and light.

Ye are the salt of the earth: but if the salt have lost his savour, wherewith shall it be salted? it is henceforth good for nothing, but to be cast out, and to be trodden under foot of men. Ye are the light of the world. A city that is set on a hill cannot be hid. Neither do men light a candle, and put it under a bushel, but on a candlestick; and it giveth light unto all that are in the house. Let your light so shine before men, that they may see your good works, and glorify your Father which is in heaven.

(Matthew 5:13-16)

11

The Salt and the Light

Salt and light are commodities that we take for granted, but in the ancient world they were greatly valued. The Roman soldiers were given their salt rations and would revolt if those rations were changed. Our English word *salary* literally means "salt money." The next time you say, "That man is not worth his salt," you are reminding yourself of the value that people put on salt back in those days.

We flick a switch and have as much light as we need; but the Jews that Jesus ministered to had to carry little clay dishes with oil and wicks if they wanted light. When one of our cities experiences a power failure, we wake up to the fact that light is important; but usually we take it for granted.

Jesus used salt and light as pictures of the Christian. No doubt He was describing the disciples particularly, since He changed from the third person in the Beatitudes to the second person in these verses. But to apply these truths only to "Christian workers" would rob us of the blessing and rob the world of the ministry that every believer can perform. In the Beatitudes, our Lord was de-

scribing Christian character; and now in these two illustrations He showed what this character means in everyday life. By using the images of salt and light, He gave us
some valuable insights into what it means to be a Christian today.

THE WONDER OF SALVATION

He first gave us an insight into our own salvation.
When we trusted Christ, a miracle took place. We became "partakers of the divine nature" (2 Peter 1:4) so
that a new ingredient was added to our lives. Clay became salt! And darkness became light: "For ye were
sometimes darkness, but now are ye light in the Lord"
(Ephesians 5:8).

Christians are different from unbelievers because
Christians possess the very nature of God, having been
born into His family. "God is light" (1 John 1:5), and we
are the children of light. Throughout the ancient world,
salt was a symbol of purity and faithfulness, and Jesus
Christ dared to apply this symbol to those who trust Him.
It must have shocked both the disciples and the crowd
when Jesus gave them those titles! They could understand a king or a great prophet being called "the salt of
the earth" and "the light of the world," but certainly not a
group of ordinary laymen. Still, it is true: because of the
miracle of God's grace, the Christian is salt and light—a
new ingredient has been added, and an old ingredient has
been taken away. Sin has been forgiven, the new nature
has been implanted, and the Christian stands before the
world as God's salt and light.

That means both privilege and responsibility. Along
with the dignity of our calling is the duty of our calling.
Jesus does not tell us that we should be salt and light: He
tells us that we *are* salt and light. We cannot change what
we are, but we can waste what we are: the salt can lose its

saltiness, and the light can be put under a bushel. That does not deny the miracle that changed us; it only defeats the ministry that challenges us. It would do us good to reflect from time to time on the miracle of our salvation—that clay should become salt and darkness should become light! Taking for granted this miracle of God's grace is certain to lead to spiritual decay. The wonder and glory of it must never leave our hearts. Knowing what I am in Christ enables me, by faith, to do what Christ wants me to do.

The Sermon on the Mount is an impossible enigma to the person who has never experienced this miracle. No matter how religious he may be, or how sincere, if he has never been transformed by God's power, he can never live the transformed life described in this sermon. It requires a miracle.

THE PLIGHT OF THE WORLD

Those two images also give us insight into our world. If the Christian is salt, then he is living in a *decaying* world; and if he is light, he is living in a *dark* world.

Jesus harbored no illusions about this world. To be sure, He saw His Father's creation and rejoiced in it—the lilies of the field, the sparrows, even the seeds in the sower's bag. Nowhere does the Bible condemn God's creation in spite of the fact that creation is groaning because of sin. The heavens still declare the glory of God, and the earth reveals His handiwork (Psalm 19:1). The world of creation is here for us to enjoy.

Neither did our Lord condemn the world of humanity. "For God so loved the world, that he gave his only begotten Son" (John 3:16). Sin has done terrible damage to the creature that God made in His image; but God still loves man and wants to save him. The world of creation and the world of humanity have both been ravaged by sin, but both can share in redemption. Mankind apart from Christ is lost, and Jesus came to save the lost.

It is the world that man has made that is decaying, that whole system that denies God and exalts man. When Jesus said, "They are not of the world, even as I am not of the world" (John 17:16), it was this system to which He was referring. We are in the world physically, but not of the world spiritually. Like a scuba diver in the ocean, the believer is out of his element in this present world system because his citizenship is in heaven. The world is a vast graveyard spiritually, and Christians are the only people who are really alive! Jesus looked upon the world as a decaying corpse when He said, "Wheresoever the body is, thither will the eagles be gathered together" (Luke 17:37). And Peter described this world system as "a dark place" (2 Peter 1:19). The word translated "dark" means "squalid" or "murky," which hardly pictures this world as a paradise.

Decay, of course, is caused by death. When a living creature dies, it can no longer support its cell structure, so the body begins to decompose. When God created the world and the first man and woman, everything pulsated with life. When sin invaded, death entered the scene, and with death came decay. From a physical point of view, decay became a blessing, because it removes unwanted dead matter and turns it into useful soil; but from a spiritual point of view, decay is disaster. It is evidence of spiritual death: mankind is separated from God.

We see decay in every area of life. Centuries ago, the prophet Daniel saw the meaning of the image and revealed the fact that the political world would decay—from gold to silver, to brass, and then to iron and clay. History started with clay, and it will end with clay. Certainly the religious world is decaying: men have a "form of godliness," but there is no power (2 Timothy 3:5). "Nevertheless when the Son of man cometh, shall he find faith on the earth?" (Luke 18:8). One does not have to take a survey to learn that moral standards have decayed. The "perilous times" that Paul warned about are certainly here (2 Timothy 3:1-5).

When things decay, they fall apart, and we are seeing society fall apart around us. Marriages have a difficult time staying together, and families are being scattered. Law and order are laughed at, and the basic institutions of society are threatened with extinction. On the outside, some of the structures look sound; but inside they are rotting away, and it is only a matter of time before they fall. The corpse is rotting away, and the eagles are gathering together.

Not only is it a decaying world, but it is a dark world, in spite of the fact that we claim to be enlightened. There is a great deal of knowledge and little wisdom. Intellectual darkness pervades our educational systems because God has been asked to leave. "Because that, when they knew God, they glorified him not as God, neither were thankful; but became vain in their imaginations, and their foolish heart was darkened" (Romans 1:21). History is not an account of evolution, with man climbing higher; it is a sad tale of devolution, with man turning his back on the heights and plunging to the depths. Man is not looking for the light; he has rejected the light and is walking in the shadows into deeper and deeper darkness. Man's very light is darkness! "If therefore the light that is in thee be darkness, how great is that darkness!" (Matthew 6:23).

Darkness and decay go together. Because there is political darkness ("We will not have this man to reign over us!"), the governments of the world are decaying. Because there is religious darkness, the religions of the world are falling apart and desperately trying to save themselves by joining together. And because there is moral darkness, it is not safe to walk the streets even in the daytime. "For behold, the darkness shall cover the earth, and gross darkness the people" (Isaiah 60:2).

This darkness and decay help to explain why people are confused. Nothing looks right in the dark. You can see shapes, but not sizes and appearances. Everything is distorted in the dark. Is it any wonder that values are twisted and distorted with the world so shrouded in darkness? Gold is more important than goodness, things are more important than people, and God is not important at all. No wonder people stumble and fall! No wonder men cannot tell their friends from their enemies! When Jesus Christ was on earth, the light was shining. "As long as I am in the world, I am the light of the world" (John 9:5). He warned them: "Yet a little while is the light with you. Walk while ye have the light, lest darkness come upon you: for he that walketh in darkness knoweth not whither he goeth" (John 12:35).

Is there any hope for a dark, decaying world?

THE CHALLENGE OF MINISTRY

The third insight that our Lord gave us is into our own position and ministry in this world. The world is decaying, but Christians are salt. The world is dark, but Christians are light.

Salt, of course, hinders corruption. The fact that the world is decaying should not encourage the Christian to isolate and insulate himself, or to stand on the sidelines and wait for the great collapse. The contrast between Jonah and Jesus illustrates the point: Jonah sat outside the city and hoped that judgment would fall, whereas Jesus looked upon the city and wept over it because judgment was inevitable. Sometimes we Christians not only hate sin, but we hate sinners! Abraham knew how corrupt Sodom was, yet he prayed that the city might be spared. Paul knew how blind Israel was, yet he was willing to be accursed that Israel might be saved. Joseph in Egypt and Daniel in Babylon both acted as divine salt in the midst of a corrupt society, and God used them. Their ministries did not prevent the ultimate collapse of the nations, but those men did stand for God and leave the nations without excuse.

If the world is as corrupt as it is with Christians present in it, what will civilization be like when the Christians are gone? Little does the world system realize that it is the presence of God's people that prevents that final collapse and that ultimate judgment. Lot was anything but a dedicated believer, yet his presence in Sodom made it impossible for God to judge the city. His presence in Zoar spared the city; his absence from Sodom condemned the city. One day God will judge this present world system, but He must call His own out of it before that judgment can fall. Meanwhile, our responsibility is to exert all the power we can to prevent decay and to win people to Christ. That does not mean that we must live like the world in order to influence the world. Abraham, separated from Sodom, actually had more influence on the city than did Lot, who was living in Sodom. And he did the city more good! When the kings captured Lot and the rest of the citizens, it was Abraham who rescued them. By risking his life to save them, Abraham gave them more witnesses in one night than Lot had given them in years. And when Abraham refused to accept the offer of the king of Sodom, he witnessed to the whole city that his faith was in the true God. Lot, immersed in the activities of the sinful city, had no influence upon his own family; yet Abraham, the friend of God, exerted a powerful influence as he interceded for the lost.

Salt not only hinders corruption but it also seasons whatever it touches. The world is a better place for the presence of Christians, whether the world admits it or not. If we were to take out of civilization the influence of

Christian thought and Christian people, little would be left. This is not to say that only Christians have made lasting contributions to society, because many unbelievers have contributed much that is of value. But it is because of the fruits of the Christian message that mankind has the freedom and the dignity to pursue truth. Even modern science, which may scoff at the gospel, is a result of the gospel. When God gave man dominion, He gave him His mandate to search and discover and invent. The furniture of the house of civilization comes from many different hands, but the foundation was laid by God.

When salt touches an open wound, it stings. Christians are not honey to soothe a sinful world; they are salt to convict it. The presence of the Holy Spirit in the church, witnessing through the world, convicts the world "of sin, and of righteousness, and of judgment" (John 16:8). That is one reason the world hates us. "If I had not come and spoken unto them, they had not had sin: but now they have no cloak for their sin" (John 15:22).

Salt makes people thirsty. If we are truly the salt of the earth, people will see in us what they are seeking for themselves and will want to take hold of it. Jesus attracted all kinds of needy people—and so should the dedicated Christian. The lost may not agree with our theology, or even our way of life, but they will see in us qualities that they lack themselves and would like to possess. The Pharisees repelled the publicans and sinners, but Jesus attracted them. He made them thirsty for what He alone could give. The more we are like Him, the more sinners will be attracted by our life and witness as we are the salt of the earth.

But we are also the light of the world. Jesus defined this light as "good works." As salt, we must have the kind of character that penetrates and purifies, and as light, we must have the kind of conduct that points to God. We like to think of these good works as religious works, but Jesus did not define them that way. Good works are simply works motivated by love, energized by the Spirit, and done to the glory of God. "For it is God which worketh in you both to will and to do of his good pleasure" (Philippians 2:13). Unsaved people certainly can perform good deeds, but these are not like the Spirit-directed good works that come from the lives of God's people. Too often good deeds point to the doer; but the good works Jesus talked about point to God.

Once again, we must avoid extremes. There are those who believe they have not served God unless they have preached a sermon or given out a piece of Christian literature. There are others who reject that kind of service and think only of the "practical" things of life, such as healing the sick and feeding the hungry. Social action sometimes replaces evangelism. Actually, our good works glorify God only if they begin with God and are empowered by His Spirit. Jesus said of the Holy Spirit, "He shall glorify me" (John 16:14). Whether we are giving a neighbor a ride to the store, helping a child with his lessons, or teaching a Sunday school class, if our works are motivated by love and empowered by the Spirit, they will point others to God. There are no such categories as religious works and secular works, for the Christian is to "do all to the glory of God" (1 Corinthians 10:31). The missionary doctor heals the body, that he might demonstrate God's love and eventually have the privilege of helping to heal the soul. The Christian neighbor helps those around him, not simply to win the right to be heard, but because showing Christian love is in itself a ministry to the glory of God.

Salt and light balance each other. Salt is hidden: it works secretly and slowly. Light is seen: it works openly and quickly. The influence of Christian character is quiet and penetrating. The influence of Christian conduct is obvious and attracting. The two go together and reinforce each other. Conduct without character is hypocrisy; character without conduct is disobedience. A church officer once told me, "I don't go around the shop doing a lot of good works. I just let my light shine for the Lord." But the way to let your light shine is to do good works! And those good works must be backed up with true character, the kind that is described in the Beatitudes.

Both salt and light must make contact if they are to do any good. Salt in the container can never have any influence, neither can a light hidden under a bushel. Too many Christians have the idea that they are serving God by sitting in church, when the greatest needs are outside the church building. We fellowship with God's people, that we might receive the grace needed to serve Christ out in the world. Worship builds character, and character leads to conduct. Separation from sin does not mean isolation from sinners. The salt must make contact if it is to do any good, and the light must be seen. Why is it that so few believers dare to make this contact? The answer to that question leads us to the fourth insight that Jesus gave us.

THE DANGERS AHEAD

The Lord gave us insight into the dangers that are involved when you and I attempt to be salt and light in this world. There is, first of all, the danger that the salt might lose its saltiness and become good for nothing. Our modern salt would not lose its flavor, because it is highly refined; but back in Jesus' day, salt did lose its flavor. William Thompson, in his classic work *The Land and the Book,* tells about merchant who rented several houses in which he stored salt. The merchant, however, forgot to cover the dirt floors of the houses and simply unloaded the salt directly on the earth. When he returned many days later, he discovered that his salt had lost its flavor from being next to the ground. The entire supply was actually thrown into the street, where men walked upon it.

The Christian is not yet perfect; there is still that old nature within that can cause him to sin. The greatest problem we face in serving Christ is having contact with sinners without being contaminated by sin. Jesus Christ was the friend of publicans and sinners, yet He was "holy, harmless, undefiled, separate from sinners" (Hebrews 7:26). There was contact without contamination; there was true separation without insulation or isolation. Only the Spirit of God can keep us from losing our flavor as we seek to minister to the lost. Of course, this loss of flavor would be a gradual thing. First there is friendship with the world (James 4:4), and then we are spotted by the world (see James 1:27). This leads to a love for the world (1 John 2:15) and then conformity to the world (Romans 12:2). By then, the salt has lost its flavor and is good for nothing.

We must also beware of the light's being hidden. Only we can hide our lights. The religious leaders tried to hide the lights of the apostles, but the more the lights were threatened, the brighter they blazed. The history of the church is the story of the light shining in the darkness and the darkness trying to put it out (John 1:5). Our Lord was not talking about a person losing his salvation, because such an experience is not possible. His subject was witnessing, glorifying God by the lives that we live. Unless the wick of witness is fed by the oil of the Holy Spirit, the light will go out. "But ye shall receive power, when the Holy Ghost is come upon you, and ye shall be witnesses unto me" (Acts 1:8, literal translation).

It is worth noting that Jesus put the lamp on the lampstand ("candlestick") where it could give light "to all the house." If our light is going to shine at all, it will shine first at home. The man out of whom Jesus cast the legion of demons wanted to go with the Lord and serve Him, but Jesus told him: "Go home to thy friends, and tell them how great things the Lord hath done for thee, and hath had compassion on thee" (Mark 5:19). We think that the greatest darkness is the farthest away, when it may be right at home. And the light that shines brightly at home will reach people away from home.

In these days of mass movements and great organizations, we tend to belittle the witness of one person. "What can a little salt do to influence a whole world?" we ask. "What good is a little candle when the world is so dark?" And yet the emphasis in the Bible is on the work and witness of *one person.* When human history was at its darkest after the Flood, God called one man, Abraham, and this one man has blessed the whole world. When Israel was experiencing its darkest hour in Egypt, God called one man, Moses, and the result was freedom. God has always had His man waiting in the wings when it seemed impossible for the drama of history to finish on a note of victory.

God is still looking for people who will be salt and light. It is a difficult and dangerous ministry, but it is an essential one. Salt and light must give of themselves so that others might be helped, and what they do is usually taken for granted. But whether or not the salt and light are noticed is really not important. The important thing is that men glorify God.

Books by Warren W. Wiersbe

In Praise of Plodders
Plodders are those who labor with determination and drive—whether pastor, teacher, choir director, or counselor. Drawing on years of ministry experience, Dr. Wiersbe offers sound advice and workable solutions to problems encountered by those who minister.
ISBN 0-8254-4048-3   144 pp.   paperback

Treasury of the World's Great Sermons
These 122 outstanding sermons are presented from 122 of the greatest preachers. A short biographical sketch of every preacher is also included. Complete with an index of texts and of sermons.
ISBN 0-8254-4002-5   672 pp.   paperback

Kregel Classic Sermons Series

Classic Sermons on the Attributes of God
ISBN 0-8254-4038-6   160 pp.   paperback

Classic Sermons on the Birth of Christ
ISBN 0-8254-4044-0   160 pp.   paperback

Classic Sermons on Christian Service
ISBN 0-8254-4041-6   160 pp.   paperback

Classic Sermons on the Cross of Christ
ISBN 0-8254-4040-8   160 pp.   paperback

Classic Sermons on Faith and Doubt
ISBN 0-8254-4028-9   160 pp.   paperback

Classic Sermons on Family and Home
ISBN 0-8254-4054-8   160 pp.   paperback

Classic Sermons on Heaven and Hell
ISBN 0-8254-3995-7   160 pp.   paperback

Classic Sermons on Hope
ISBN 0-8254-4045-9   160 pp.   paperback

Classic Sermons on the Names of God
ISBN 0-8254-4052-1   160 pp.   paperback

Classic Sermons on Overcoming Fear
ISBN 0-8254-4043-2   160 pp.   paperback

Classic Sermons on Praise
ISBN 0-8254-3994-9   160 pp.   paperback

Classic Sermons on Prayer
ISBN 0-8254-4029-7   160 pp.   paperback

Classic Sermons on the Prodigal Son
ISBN 0-8254-4039-4   160 pp.   paperback

Classic Sermons on the Resurrection of Christ
ISBN 0-8254-4042-4   160 pp.   paperback

Classic Sermons on the Second Coming and Other Prophetic Themes
ISBN 0-8254-4051-3   160 pp.   paperback

Classic Sermons on the Sovereignty of God
ISBN 0-8254-4055-6   160 pp.   paperback

Classic Sermons on Spiritual Warfare
ISBN 0-8254-4049-1   160 pp.   paperback

Classic Sermons on Suffering
ISBN 0-8254-4027-0   204 pp.   paperback

Classic Sermons on Worship
ISBN 0-8254-4037-8   160 pp.   paperback